## Praise for *Never Argue with a Dead Person*

"I've been to many mediums. Thomas is by far the most accurate one. Spot on!"

—Jenny McCarthy, actress

"Thomas John's way with words will hit home with everyone! His loving memories of his father especially made me smile and I could relate. Living with this ability is what you make of it and Thomas has chosen to use his wisely!"

—Concetta Bertoldi, author of *Do Dead People Watch You In The Shower?*

"Reading Thomas John's *Never Argue with A Dead Person* is like having a best friend who's a great storyteller and happens to be able to commune with the dead; endlessly fascinating and thoroughly enjoyable."

—Monte Farber & Amy Zerner, authors of *The Soulmate Path*, *The Enchanted Tarot*, and *Quantum Affirmations*

"Thomas John is one of the most gifted psychic mediums working today. His book is a lively, entertaining, and informative account of his work with the other side. I recommend it highly."

—Paul Selig, author of *The Book of Knowing and Worth: A Channeled Text*

"No one has consistently amazed me more than the young and gifted Thomas John. His details are so acute and his information so accurate, that my listeners never cease to be astounded, comforted, and healed."

—Laura Smith, WABC radio host and media personality.

"I've written a great deal about psychics over the years—for *W* magazine, *Women's Wear Daily*, and for *The Hollywood Reporter*. Thomas John is very simply THE REAL DEAL. You don't come across that too often, Not only is he a miraculous channeler—knowing so many things from my family tree I'd forgotten myself—his psychic abilities are so accurate. They used to scare me—until I just stopped questioning them and became co-dependent. He's also warm, empathetic, a great combo of spiritual and secular, funny, and a wonderfully natural writer who penetrates deep into the souls of both the dead— and the living."

—Merle Ginsberg, *The Hollywood Reporter*

"A wonderful introduction to the Other Side. His stories delight, entertain, and inform."

—Echo Bodine, author of *The Little Book of True Ghost Stories* and *Echoes of the Soul*

"In his meticulously researched yet delightfully readable Spirit 'tell-all,' John shares healing messages from the Other Side, producing an often humorous but always authentic guide showing us how we, the living, can focus on unconditional love, gratitude, and forgiveness to manifest greater meaning, purpose, and joy in our everyday lives."

—Kathy Eldon, author and film producer

# NEVER ARGUE

WITH A

# DEAD PERSON

# NEVER ARGUE

## WITH A

# DEAD PERSON

True and
Unbelievable
Stories from the
Other Side

## THOMAS JOHN

HAMPTON ROADS

Cover design by Jim Warner
Author photo on cover by Daniel D'Ottavio *www.danieldottavio.com*
Interior designed by Deborah Dutton

Hampton Roads Publishing Company, Inc.
Charlottesville, VA 22906
Distributed by Red Wheel/Weiser, LLC
*www.redwheelweiser.com*

Sign up for our newsletter and special offers by going to
*www.redwheelweiser.com/newsletter/*.

ISBN: 978-1-57174-724-2

Library of Congress cataloging-in-publication data available upon request
Printed in the United States of America.
EBM

10 9 8 7 6 5 4 3 2 1

## DEDICATIONS

*To Rita—my grandmother, role model, biggest fan, and best friend—thank you for your eternal love. May we be reunited "over the rainbow."*

# ACKNOWLEDGMENTS

This book has been thirty years in the making. There are many people to thank.

Most importantly, I must thank my clients, who are loyal, thought-provoking, and have allowed me to hold space for them over the past seven years in my private practice doing my work as a spiritual medium. I am blessed to know each and every one of you. This is your book, and your stories, so thank you for letting the world hear the whispers of your soul. I am especially thankful to my spunky Michigan women, whom I affectionately call "The 248 ladies," especially my dear friend Anne—who five years ago told me her reading so moved her that she was going to send me one hundred new clients. Anne, I think you surpassed that number a while ago!

To my family, my mother, who has always been there for me—may you relish in the fact that you are the original "helicopter parent" and loved for it. To my sister Kelly, and her fiancé David, and my sister Kara, thank you for supporting me with love, friendship, and laughter. To my stepfather, Gerard, I am thankful for the love that you have bestowed on my mother and my family—you are a gentleman.

To my dear friend Laura Jean Smith—who has served as a loving second mother, has helped me manage and develop my career, and gave me one of my first opportunities to be in the media, I am eternally grateful. What a great bond we have shared in this lifetime and many others. May your spirit continue to be bright with wisdom and love.

To D, you are very special to me, and may we share many laughs, kisses, and beautiful memories for many years to come. Thank you for accepting me as I am, but also challenging me to grow. To my friends—ones of a lifetime and ones recent—how blessed I am to share in so many friendships that are supportive and filled with unconditional love. I hope I am half the friend you have all been to me. Humor is the great thread that brings us together. Without Steve Kopp, Josh Garcia, Daniel D'Ottavio, Marcy Cole, Jimmy Floyd, Lynne White, Joel Schnell, Francky L'Official, Chilli Pepper, Marisa May, Christina Carathanassis (and "The Family"), Jason Scarlatti and Trey Watkins, Debbie Nigro, Jennifer McCrea, Joelle Soliman, Pam Linehan, Eileen Brown, and Heide Banks, I'd have a lot more dead friends than I do living friends. Thanks for allowing me to have one foot in this world. To my great spiritual teachers, and those in the community that

I deeply respect, I hold so many of you on such a high pedestal—including Jodi Serota, John Edward, Jeffrey Wands, Rita Berkowitz, Zenobia Simmons, Donnaleigh de La Rose, Paul Selig, Terry and Linda Jamison, Monte Farber, Amy Zerner, and Echo Bodine. You have all taught me either directly or by example.

To Bert Cohler, my first teacher in many ways, thank you. Your memory lives on.

To my tireless assistants—Donna McDine Barbie Schassler, and and my sisters Kelly and Kara—I am not sure where I would be without you. Likely in a very disorganized state. Thank you for always keeping me on track. Thank you also to Giselle Ross who has always been willing to lend a helping hand.

To my professional relationships with my publicists, who have worked fearlessly and tirelessly to support my career and gain me access to opportunities to share my work with a broader audience. I am thankful to Lisa Schneidermann, Norah Lawlor, and Nancy Kane. I am also especially thankful to the many writers, producers, and celebrity clients—including Merle Ginsberg, Celeste McLaughlin, Carla Pennington, Michelle Wendt, Eileen Cope, Adam Block, Jenny McCarthy, Sonja Tremont-Morgan, Courtney Cox, and Anne Radecki. Thank you for putting me on the map.

To my team at Hampton Roads Publishing, especially Greg Brandenburgh and Bonni Hamilton, thank you for giving me this opportunity. Also, thank you to Margaret Santangelo and Alix Strauss for reading multiple drafts of the book.

And last, but not least, thank you to the dead people. For where would a medium be without dead people? Thank you for your continual guidance and words of wisdom. I'm always listening.

May we all laugh and love in this lifetime and continue to on the Other Side.

# CONTENTS

Introduction      xxi

**CHAPTER 1**
The Case of the Missing Watch      1

**CHAPTER 2**
Time Out      13

**CHAPTER 3**
Teaching Mommy      29

**CHAPTER 4**
"Young Hearts Run Free"                                    43

**CHAPTER 5**
Hockey Goal                                                53

**CHAPTER 6**
Tony                                                       67

**CHAPTER 7**
The Two Dads                                               77

**CHAPTER 8**
Maternal Love                                              87

**CHAPTER 9**
There's Chocolate and Champagne in Heaven                  93

**CHAPTER 10**
"Luck Be a Lady Tonight"                                   105

**CHAPTER 11**
"Murder, She Wrote"                                        121

**CHAPTER 12**
House for Sale                                          139

**CHAPTER 13**
"And Now You Know the Rest of the Story"               155

**CHAPTER 14**
Dying to Believe                                        171

**CHAPTER 15**
Wanted: Dead or Alive                                   191

## A NOTE FROM THE AUTHOR

This book accurately reflects my experiences as a psychic and medium, but I have changed names, identifying details and locations of both the living and the dead.

# LIVING WITH THE DEAD

"It's not that I'm afraid to die. I just don't want to be there when it happens."

—Woody Allen

"SLAM." I still remember waking up to an unknown, deafening sound, alone in my room at the age of four. I lay quietly in my bed, staring up at the ceiling towards the glow-in-the-dark stickers that had absorbed the daylight and transformed it into an alien green glow that shone down upon me. I wore red pajamas, with white feet. One of the feet had a small hole in it, and my toe popped out of it.

I pulled my flashlight out from under my bed and waved it in the air. My dad let me use it so I could play shadow puppets if I got scared or nervous being alone. "That way," he would tell me, "you won't come waking me up." Feeling protected in the bunkbed fortress that my uncle had built for me, I peeked around the headboard post.

Shining the light toward my closet, I saw an image—an image I will never forget. It was dark and foggy; it looked like a bunch of light had formed into an image or a picture. The man was dressed just the way I had seen him in many of our old photographs. I immediately recognized him; I didn't even have to think. I just knew, almost as if I had been waiting for him to appear. I felt like I had prepared for this moment every second of my short four years on this Earth.

"Puppa!" I said out loud.

I wasn't scared; I wasn't surprised. I remember just sitting there—in awe.

Then, in a deep voice, I heard, "Jack has my watch, boy. Tell Mom and Dad. I love you." He vanished just after making this cryptic statement.

Immediately, I heard my parents' bedroom door opening. Within a second or two, as I stood in the middle of my bedroom, my father flung open the door. "What the hell is going on in here?" he said, standing only in tube socks and boxer shorts.

"Puppa come!" I said out loud, "Puppa come."

"You saw Puppa?" my father asked in a gruff voice. "Boy, what the hell are you talking about?"

I started crying. My dad approached me and picked me up into his arms. He gave me a kiss on the cheek. That was my father's way—he'd snap and then apologize. "It's okay, son. Weird things happen at night."

And so began my life as a psychic medium—a seer, a soothsayer, a mystic. But what I learned—almost immediately—is that weird things do not *only* happen at night: they happen all the time, and they happen to *me* on an almost continual basis. I quickly learned—at the age of four—that while the dead may be dead, they still have a lot to say, and it is my job to listen. As kids, we all learn to look both ways and never take candy from a stranger. I also learned to never argue with a dead person—they often know more than the living.

As a psychic medium, I have two particular abilities. First, as a psychic, I have visions about the future, in which I can see where people have come from and where they are going. Second, I connect with the Spirits of those that have departed. Taken together, it's a combination of hearing a lot of voices and seeing a lot of things. People are amazed by it, obsessed by it, confused by it, and always intrigued by it. It's the best and worst profession to have at a cocktail party— people either want to talk to you all night or run from you like the plague. But I'm not here to make you believe in the reality of psychic mediums. I am not here to convince you of the afterlife. Actually, I'm really not even here to tell you about myself (even though I am writing this book). This is the story of those that have passed on—those that have left us, but continue to guide us and love us in some way. This is the story of my clients who have come to me over the years and opened up their hearts to hear from beyond, and have trusted me to shepherd them along the way. This is a book about the fun, anecdotal stories that reveal the tremendous healing power of connecting with the Other Side—with our "team spirit"—of angels, loved ones, and guides.

There are a lot of unbelievable stories and life-altering experiences that accompany this work. Recounting experiences and answering the questions (as best I can) are the main impetus behind my writing this book. You will learn a lot about my life and work through this book, but ultimately, I hope that you will take the lessons that each deceased person brings forward in this book and use them to inspire you on your own path in life. Now, you might be thinking, *Wait a second—I'm reading a whole book about other people's dead people? Boring!* but let me stop you right there. This is not a book about dead people. This is a book about the universal lessons, messages, and healing that we all wish for in our lives.

People on the Other Side come through for a variety of reasons. First, they deliver a message to validate they are indeed in the Spirit World. They do this by bringing through identifying details like names, dates, and information about their lives that the person sitting with me can relate to. However, in many ways, while this is the most exciting part of the reading—mainly because it defies our logical minds—it could perhaps be the most useless in terms of resolving important issues that propelled you to seek a reading. The reason is simply that this "confirmation" of information is often stuff that you *already* know, such as specific memories or significant names and details.

While conformational messages fortify and confirm the connection, they do not serve to provide spiritual growth or inspire a change in my clients' life journeys. A whole different, and much more significant, class of information can be brought about when Spirit comes through and connects to living loved ones: *to teach them a valuable life lesson.* These life

lessons can be about unconditional love, gratefulness, seren-
dipity, and forgiveness. The dead can teach us a lot about life
on Earth and can guide us in many ways. For many of us, we
constantly obsess about the past: what we should have done,
could have done, or would have done. We dated the wrong
person, married the wrong person, spent too much money, or
took the wrong job. When something terrible happens, we
become guilt-ridden instead of understanding that through
this trauma, positive developments can happen—if we allow
them. But the dead have a very different version of Earth—
they view it as our classroom and playground—where everything is in the name of learning, and every experience we
endure (positive or negative) can teach us a very important
life lesson.

When people leave their physical bodies, their Spirit is
able to see life and life's problems from an entirely new perspective. After achieving this clarity, our loved ones' Spirits
are excited and eager to help us with their new knowledge.
But they also move on. They move past the relatively common
things that we become obsessed with in life. People often ask,
"Are they always around us?" and the answer is a bit confusing, because it is both yes and no. I sometimes like to joke
that the dead have lives too, and they can't be everywhere
all the time. The truth is, they are around us a lot, but often,
they are doing their own thing. They have many duties and
responsibilities on the Other Side (many Spirits have come
through in readings to me and told me about their Spirit
World jobs, but that is another story). One thing I do know
is that in the thousands of readings I've conducted—whether
it be in groups, one-on-one at my Chelsea office, or over the

telephone, I have learned that they want to communicate with us. In fact, they actually enjoy the connection. And the reason they connect is that they love us. Connecting helps us, but it also helps them. It is part of their "job" on the Other Side: teaching the living lessons enables these Spirits to progress to higher dimensions. This book is about those sacred lessons and universal messages.

Another common question—probably the most common of all—"Do you see dead people?" The answer is yes, generally, but I also sometimes don't. It depends a lot on how the Spirits from the other side want to communicate. They might communicate through signs and symbols, through images related to their lives, and through personal experiences. Often, they also do communicate through showing themselves in the physical body. So I do "see" dead people, but I also see images, feel sensations, and hear sounds that help me create a story about who I am connecting with and what they wish to communicate.

In this book, you won't find many references to *super consciousness* and *chakras*, *channeling*, and other psychic mumbo-jumbo. I've decided to keep it simple and honest. I candidly share with you fifteen stories from my practice as one of Manhattan's top psychic mediums—and every one of them has a message from a dead person. Some are touching (like a mother who came through to forgive her daughter who had accidentally killed her), some are creepy (like the woman who got a message from her husband whom she thought was living and meeting her for dinner after the reading), some are totally unbelievable (like a young couple who bonded over their fathers' deaths), but all are true accounts of my encounters with the departed. Some happen in my Chelsea office, some happen at the Rite Aid I frequent, on the corner of 19th and 8th Avenue, and some happen on the A train after a long night in the meatpacking district. Some are predictable, and some will surprise you. I hope you laugh, and you might cry or be confused—but I'll try to make it as easy as possible as we go on this journey together.

I hope you enjoy this book, but whatever your reaction, believers and skeptics alike, I hope you'll agree the dead have a lot to say. This book is filled with true yet unbelievable moments when even I stop and say: "Is this for real?" And even though the stories might be about someone else's dead aunt or crossed-over grandmother, the messages that they have for their loved ones are ones that we all can bear witness to, understand, and heal from. This isn't about the specific message, story, or character that conveys something about our loved ones. Instead, it's about the lesson in the connection for all of us. For some, seeing is believing, but for me, it is the opposite: *believing is seeing.* Hopefully, by reading this book, you will believe and understand the Other Side. And if there's one thing I have learned about dead people, it's that they have a lot to say, and they're usually right—so don't argue with a dead person!

# CHAPTER 1

# THE CASE OF THE MISSING WATCH

"And above all, watch with glittering eyes the whole world around you because the greatest secrets are always hidden in the most unlikely places. Those who don't believe in magic will never find it."

—Roald Dahl

During my childhood, I remember my grandfather as a handsome guy, in a very striking sort of way. He was tall, skinny, and wore flannel shirts all the time. His clothes were simple—his plaid flannel shirt, broken-in blue jeans, and always a pair of well-worn, thick-soled, leather work boots. The skin of his face was tired and stretched. His eyes were bloodshot, perhaps reflecting the stress during his years as an officer in the army, or maybe it was the strain of his unhappy marriage to my alcoholic grandmother. He had a thick head of hair, with only a few gray patches on the sides. He had regrets—the affair he had had all through my father's childhood and the fact that he emotionally could never trust anyone. His presence was quiet. He had a way of walking into a room and immediately being seen and then as quickly disappearing. We met the first time when I was the tender age of four. When we saw each other, it was always at night. He would come to my bedroom, speak quietly to me for a few minutes, and then leave. I am the only person to whom he ever said: "I love you." To say that my relationship with my grandfather is unconventional is an understatement, to say the least. But what makes it all even stranger is this: my grandfather, Leo, passed away five years before my birth.

My grandfather was a hard worker, of the blue-collar variety. A career electrician, he rarely missed a day of work over his thirty-five-year-long tenure with the union. He led a fairly uninteresting life. He was never happy in his marriage, and had many affairs with women, and drank many of his fears and anxieties away at the bar. Because of this, his relationship with my father suffered. But we never really spoke about these things in our family. My grandfather died after battling cancer two years before my parents were married, and my grandfather became little more than a memory in an 8-by-10 photo. Leo didn't like to take photographs, and only a few black-and-white pictures of him survived. My grandfather wasn't discussed much at reunions or family gatherings. Any of my relatives' accounts of him paint him as a hard-working type of guy, up early every morning; the type who believed only after a full twelve hours of labor did one deserve to sleep. He served in the army for four years, an experience that made him formidable in the way he disciplined my father. In life, he was described as a quiet man of few words, who kept to himself. He did drink heavily, but wasn't a belligerent or mean drunk. "He was a quiet drunk, but a drunk he was," my cousin, his niece Mary, would comment dryly, when reminiscing during annual family excursions to her small home in upstate New York.

As a young boy, I experienced vivid dreams. The visceral colors, senses, and emotions in my dreams were very much real to me. I did have normal dreams like everyone else, ones where I would wake up and remember surreal details, maybe a vivid scene or two that stuck with me for hours after awaking. But often, perhaps once a week, I would have a wild, vibrant dream where I saw brighter colors, bigger shapes, sharper sensations, and more primal feelings than usual; these dreams seemed to be coming from a different dimension.

My parents recall that, as a child, I would awaken, even as young as age three or four, to stir them out of their slumber and insist on recounting my dreams to them, right then and there. The dreams, my mother would later tell me, seemed unnatural and strange—they were so specific and all too real. I would describe every detail, every color, and articulate the details in a vocabulary far advanced of a four-year-old. Sometimes, I would describe the people I encountered, usually family members who had recently died or relatives who were about to cross over. My parents found this bizarre. By the age of seven, I had been to every psychotherapist, priest, rabbi, and anyone else my parents could think of to help me. Many of them actually encouraged me to talk to the "dead people." Even a Roman Catholic priest—whom my family visited when I was ten—affirmed that the Bible was, in fact, written by "special people," also known as "mystics" and "seers," and that there are, in fact, gifted people who can communicate with the dead. "It's the Angels talking to you," Father Michael told me.

My grandfather was the first to visit me, and to this day he continues to appear in my bedroom, late at night. Our connection is, now, vastly different. These days, his visits are more about his checking up on me or gracing me with a simple hello. When he first came to visit, I did not understand his intentions. At first, I mistook it for a dream. I did not yet realize it was different, or rather, that I was different. During his first few social calls, my grandfather didn't say much. I remember being comforted by a vision of him, feeling a warmth come over my chest. As time went on, he started to relate specific messages. He told me about his estate and how my grandmother's handling of what he had left behind disturbed and upset him. Another time, he passed on a message about my grandmother's health, which proved true the following day. My grandfather had many secrets and now, in retrospect, I think he visited me at a such a young age because he needed a cathartic means of ridding himself of these secrets. He wanted someone to know who he was, because for his fifty-seven years on Earth, nobody really knew.

One night, I woke up my parents to tell them that Grandpa Leo was in my bedroom. This had been going on for the past couple of years—a visit by my grandfather in the middle of the night, me waking my parents, them coming into my room only to find my assertions unsubstantiated. My mother muttered, "This is getting to be too much." I shared with them that Puppa was confused about why Jack had ended up with his prized wristwatch, despite the fact that he had wanted his wife to have it. That watch held significant meaning to my father, who had purchased a Rolex for Leo and inscribed it "To Dad, Love Tom" (yes, I am a junior, named after my father). I sleepily said something about "a donkey bank," asked if I could have a drink of water, and then asked to be put back to bed.

My parents were dumbfounded. Jack was my grandfather's best friend. I had mentioned the watch before, but this was the first time that I had mentioned Jack. He and my grandfather had worked together at the electric company for sixteen years. The mention of the donkey bank was chilling, and nobody could make sense of it for a month, until my Great Aunt Rose came for a visit and told us an unsolicited story about my late grandfather's treasured possession—a bank in the shape of a donkey that she had found in her attic the preceding week. My parents searched for this wristwatch high and low for years. It was the *one* personal item of my grandfather's that my father actually wanted, but three days after his death, it mysteriously went missing.

My grandfather, who had come back from the grave in Spirit to tell us the exact location of this watch, was completely ignored. Yet, my parents *still* refused to believe.

It would be years until they finally saw the error of their ways.

Flash forward several years. Jack came to my sister's seventh birthday party. Although he lived an hour away, he often frequented family events, staying in touch with us with the occasional holiday or birthday card. My parents affectionately called them "the odd couple." Jack was the diametric opposite of my grandfather in so many ways. Jack was short, Leo was tall; Jack was well groomed, my grandfather was somewhat sloppy and disheveled; Jack had striking dark eyes that jumped out at you, Leo had gray-blue eyes that sunk deeply into his skull; Jack was liberal, whereas my grandfather was conservative. However dissimilar they may have been, Jack had a deep, intuitive understanding of Leo. Jack was the only person who really appreciated Leo, something my grandfather told Jack before passing away.

Jack brought my sister a Barbie doll and Wizard of Oz hair clips thoughtfully yet awkwardly wrapped in white tissue paper for her birthday. As the party progressed, it transformed from a seven-year-old's party into a completely different scene. The men sat around a card table drinking beer and smoking cigars, while the women gathered in the kitchen gossiping about the latest PTA meeting as they sliced up an Entenmann's Danish. I observed the cigar smoke–filled vista quietly from my vantage point lying on the den floor.

At a certain point, my grandfather's name was mentioned. It wasn't uncommon that Leo's name usually came up when Jack was around. The men reminisced about his flannel shirts and how he had only three in rotation, which he washed only occasionally. Someone brought up how he hated animals, yet one time he took in a stray cat and treated it like royalty. They fondly remembered his contempt for Democrats and how politics was about the only thing that got him talking. "Leo was tough on those liberals," Ricky, the son of my grandfather's friend, chimed in from across the table. Cards hit the table one after another. Someone was out of beer, and there was talk about getting another six-pack from Cumby's and switching to Texas Hold 'em. Then, out of nowhere, there was a dramatic, palpable shift in the air. The smoke cleared. The room fell silent. Then I saw it, the faintest image of my grandfather, stooping down next to me on the floor. "Watch this," he whispered, his face inches from mine, just floating, ephemerally, like a slide projection of an old photograph lingering in the dusty, smoke-filled air. I looked up expectantly, holding my breath, looking back and forth from the ghostly apparition beside me to the seemingly completely unaware men and women carrying on with the business of the party just a few feet away.

A second later a loud voice boomed from the poker table. "Can't believe I still got that Rolex," Jack chuckled. "Only thing he gave a damn about was that Rolex, eh Tommy?"

All the color drained from my father's now ashen face. "Yes," my father acknowledged. "Who wants another beer? Mickey? Can I get ya another?" My father, visibly shaken, left the table abruptly, accidentally knocking over a glass of water in the process.

My father immediately went to the kitchen, but he did not make the usual bee line for the refrigerator, opening the door to get another beer while simultaneously grabbing the bottle opener to open it, in his beer retrieval ritual dance. Instead, he seemed disoriented and confused, rubbing his hand over his head quizzically. He did not open the refrigerator; in fact, he didn't move at all. He wasn't doing anything in the kitchen. He just stood there, scratching his head. Then he walked right by me, tiny beads of perspiration now covering his furrowed brow. His complexion grew a deep red, like after he'd had a few, but this time it was darker and deeper and covered his entire face. He was flustered, a state unfamiliar to my experiences of my father. My gaze left the Uno game on the floor and instead was focused on my father in the kitchen. I crawled to the doorway between the den and kitchen and poked my head through the beaded curtains to get a better view. My father spoke in a hushed, forceful tone with my mother, waving and flailing, and nervously pacing back and forth, feet stomping angrily on the vinyl tiles.

After this exchange, my father returned to the card game in the den, but the men were on to new topics. Carl was bragging about his wife's new job at the attorney general's office. Jack sipped on a bottle of beer and complained about problems with his '84 Mazda 323. My mother quickly came and went, sheepishly placing a bowl of cashews on the table without so much as a word.

The story's revelations—and finally finding the missing watch after all these years—did *not* make my parents feel any better for knowing. They were not validated or relieved by this message from my grandfather from beyond the grave. In fact, they were unnerved, almost angry.

We never did get the watch back from Jack, who ultimately passed away a few years later. The watch was nowhere to be found. I like to muse that my grandfather took the one possession he loved and treasured more than any other back to the heavens with him. To Leo, this watch represented all the qualities about himself of which he was most proud: his punctuality, his reliability, and his son.

We never again talked about that fateful night, the night that Jack revealed he had had the watch all along. My parents just weren't comfortable with the implications, though I knew that in a way, it comforted them. They couldn't wrap their heads around it. They didn't have the language to understand the events or speak about them after the fact. But it became less about the watch as a memento of my grandfather or as an antique time-keeping device and more about the watch as a symbol of my grandfather's validation of his love for his son, my father, and validation of the man as a proud, hard-working person of value.

Around my twenty-third birthday, during one of my grandfather's frequent visits, I finally just asked him straight out: "Why was it so important for you to relay a message to Dad about your Rolex? Why did you need the missing watch to be found despite the unsettling consequences of the revelation?"

"Because," he said, smiling mischievously, as his apparition, appearing as a strapping young man this visit, stood before me, "over here, there is no room between our thoughts of secrets or ideas of mysteries. We have to clear all that out. Here, where I am now, this is a world of light and clarity, such a clear sense of knowing and truth that is rarely ever experienced on Earth. Our job is to shine light into the dark corners of the lives we left behind and at least try to expose these mysteries in some way to people who may not want to know about them."

I nodded, trying to take it all in.

About a year after this conversation with my grandfather, my father and I were sharing a beer on the front porch of our family cottage in New Hampshire. We were putting together a jigsaw puzzle, an activity we occasionally enjoy sharing. I was working on the far left corner; he was working on the center. We chatted about the recent Red Sox loss and other superficial topics, nothing too deep. It was a clear night, bright twinkling stars decorated the dark blue country sky. My father took a long, deep breath, and I could see his eyes shift from the evening sky to the ground below. Out of nowhere, he blurted out: "So, you think Grandpa's okay up there?"

"I do, Dad, I do," I said, feeling a bit awkward.

"How do you know that, though?" he asked, his eyes finally meeting mine for the first time that night.

"I just do. Sometimes you don't 'know' things. Sometimes you just *feel* them. You just get a sense. . . . " I paused to think about the odd late-night visits from my grandfather, still going on, and the various messages he had passed on to me, and through me, over the years. I thought about life, about how my grandfather shaped my future fate from such an early point in my childhood. How many mysteries and puzzles he had solved, I considered them all, as the events flashed before my eyes. Life is a weird mystery—we only get the briefest time to live on the physical plane. Change is the only constant, but it is the only way to discover the many mysteries we are meant to experience in our lives. I savored this visceral connection I was experiencing between myself, my father, and my grandfather, a connection transcending time, space, life, and death, and wished in vain that it would last forever.

"That's good, son." My dad paused a long while, lighting and inhaling deeply on a cigarette. "I get what you mean." He exhaled just as deeply off to the side of the table.

The stars shone down from the heavens and warmed our souls, and in that moment, I knew, without a doubt, my grandfather was watching over us.

# CHAPTER 2

# TIME OUT

"A lot of you cared, just not enough."
                        —Jay Asher, *Thirteen Reasons Why*

Caroline Small sat patiently in my waiting room as I prepared the office to start a reading. I had been traveling for a few weeks to see friends and family, and this was my first day back in the city doing readings. Whenever I disconnect from the Other Side for a long period of time—which isn't often—I like to give myself some extra time to reacquaint with my office and surroundings, and prepare for the reading. The truth is, I'm always aware of the Spirit World, but it does shift a little bit when I am not actively giving readings to people. People often ask if I am always aware of what is around me, and if I am always seeing the Spirit World—is my day filled with a constant bombardment of dead people and messages from odd-ball Spirits? An analogy I like to use is as follows: suppose you are driving for thirty minutes. Along the way, you pass hundreds of vehicles and pedestrians in your travels—big cars, little cars, trucks, vans—who knows? If you got from Point A to Point B and someone asked "What was the color of every car you passed?" you would probably not remember. Maybe you would remember one car that really stuck out in your mind, but you wouldn't remember them all. That would be me when I am driving down the road, not trying to tune into anything. However, when I am working, I am paying attention, tuned in and very aware. So, I see more and I am aware of more—just as if you drove for thirty minutes but before you left the house, I reminded you to pay attention to what you were driving past. In that case, you would probably remember more of the vehicles that you saw.

I was saging the room and taking some extra time to pray, before I greeted Caroline. After saging, I quickly meditated and started to feel a male Spirit around her. Visually, he was a handsome guy, maybe in his thirties, with dark hair and dark eyes. His look was very well put together and his skin was a dark olive. He looked to be Greek or Italian.

"Are you here for my next client?" I asked the Spirit.

"I sure am," he said. "I'm the dead fiancé." He winked at me.

I had seen Caroline briefly as I entered my office. She had arrived early. Caroline Small was a young, thirty-something New Yorker with cropped bright blonde hair, fresh lip gloss, and well-manicured French-tip nails. She looked like the typical, successful, Upper East Side business woman. I imagined her to be a publicist or a successful account executive for a business firm. She was wearing a flower printed skirt with a white blouse and simple gold earrings. She looked like a J. Crew catalog model as she flipped through a copy of *Elle* magazine while she waited for me to greet her. Her white shoes glistened in the sunlight from the window behind her. Next to her, on the floor, was a pink and white oversized Kate Spade bag filled with magazines. When I had walked past her, she had smiled quickly and looked up from her bottle of Evian.

After I finished organizing my office, I opened the door to begin the session.

"Come on in," I said, and she got up, smiled, and walked past me into the office. "Nice to meet you!" she said enthusiastically.

This was a different type of reading than most of my work. About 80 percent of my clients seek my services to connect with deceased loved ones. Although I am a psychic and a medium, I use my skills as medium more often in my private work. However, this woman wanted to have a strictly psychic reading, and she actually made that very clear by mentioning in the "Notes" section of her appointment request that she wanted to have only a psychic reading about her future, specifically about her love life. Of course, I also knew that her dead fiancé was already visiting me, and we needed to focus the session on her healing from that situation rather than just her love life. If there's one thing I know about dead people, it's that when they show up in a reading, I have to bring them through, or they'll keep bothering me.

Immediately, I felt the man I had seen before I greeted her. He looked the same as before and was sharply dressed—a nice suit, a white shirt, no tie, shined shoes. His clothes were neatly tucked and maintained. He seemed keenly aware that he was interrupting her reading, but he felt entitled to do so. There was a degree of confidence with him that I could immediately sense. He was ready to connect and needed to be heard.

"So, I see that you are mostly looking for a psychic reading and you want to hear about your love life?" I said.

"That's correct. I really want to know when I am going to meet my soulmate and anything you can see and feel around that. I worry that I am going to be alone all my life. I feel blocked."

"Well, we can definitely do that. Are you open to hearing about anything else I might see or feel for you?" I asked, wondering how the dead person who was around her would fit into this whole situation.

"I guess so," she said with a bit of uncertainty. "I'm not sure what that means exactly."

I started to see flashes of things—bits and pieces, images in my head played out. I saw all sorts of strange scenes playing out; mostly they were scenes of this woman with her fiancé, whom I already knew had died, but I hadn't revealed this to her yet.

"Well, sometimes people come to readings thinking they are going to hear about certain things, and they end up hearing about other things. Are you open to hearing about other things that come through?" I asked.

"I guess so," she said, still sounding unsure.

And thus began the reading. I closed my eyes, said a protection prayer, and opened myself to whatever I saw or felt.

Immediately, I saw an image. "I just saw the name Florentis—like on a sign—and then I saw a restaurant. It looked Italian." I offered to her.

She smiled a bit, and then her face went quiet again without any emotion. To be honest, I thought she seemed uncomfortable.

"That's a place I know—it has to do with my fiancé that I had. But I want to focus on the future," she guided me. She stammered a bit as she spoke.

"I see. I am just trying to understand what I am seeing," I said. I could sense her nervousness.

As I tuned in, the same man who had visited me a few minutes earlier appeared. I was beginning to think this was strange because she specifically had asked not to connect with someone who was deceased. Even stranger, this man seemed to be younger, and I could sense he had passed in a tragic way. I was surprised that someone was inserting himself into a reading when the person sitting with me was clearly looking for something else entirely.

When I do a psychic reading, I rely less on the presence of deceased people for my information, and I focus mostly on getting information from what I refer to as "guides." Guides are energy beings that provide us with our highest knowledge and our inner knowledge about certain situations. They provide us with insight.

As I started to ask my guides about Caroline's love life, and her guides about her love life, I was coming up empty handed. It seemed that her guides—and my guides—didn't really want to talk about her love life. I wasn't getting any strong information. In my head, I then heard "Long way away." It was a deep whisper that emanated from my third eye.

Ugh. I definitely didn't want to give her that kind of message. She had come here asking for psychic guidance about her love life—and here I was going to tell her it was a long way away. Since so much of what I can do is subject to interpretation, I waited to tell her that until some stronger information came through. Maybe I was mishearing some things. I wanted to be careful.

"I need to speak to her," the Spirit that had appeared to me before communicated. I could hear his voice bellowing in my head.

I was starting to get anxious. We were already ten minutes into the reading, and I could feel that this woman was starting to get antsy. I was getting the wrong kind of information for her.

"Are you having trouble reading me?" she asked. She was likely confused by my hemming and hawing.

"No, I'm not having trouble reading you," I said. "I am just getting conflicting information."

"Because the time is going by really fast already," she added, looking at the clock sitting next to me. Now, she was getting irritated.

"I realize," I said. "But I want to make sure I give you the most accurate information possible."

"I need to speak to her. She won't find love until she connects with me." The Spirit that I had seen before was chiming in again.

" I really need to talk about this man that has passed away and is around you."

"I don't want anything like that; I just want messages about my love life. This is getting really frustrating," she said. "You're *not* a very good psychic."

"Look, I think I have your fiancé here. The one that died. You need to relax if you want this to work. You're yelling at me, and it is just making me more anxious," I said.

The color in her face completely left. She became pale. A tear formed in her eye and began to trickle down, and then her eyes really filled up with tears. I could tell. It became real when I went out on the line and blurted out that it was her fiancé. I wasn't playing any guessing games.

"Richard?" she said quietly.

"I am not sure of his name just yet, but there's a man here that is passed away, and he is saying that he is your fiancé that passed away in the car crash and he needs to reach you. He is saying until you get closure around this issue, you won't be able to bring in the type of love that you are wanting." I also described what he was wearing.

"That's what he was wearing the day he died. And, you know, I really do miss him," she confessed. "I never feel him around."

"So, do you want to connect with him?" I asked. "I think it might be good for you to hear some of these things."

"Is he blocking me from finding love?" she asked. "I'm just asking because we had something so special, and I feel like I compare everyone to that connection."

"He's not blocking you," I explained. "But you know, this is a pretty serious issue. He died and you need some help so that you can move forward."

She was still quiet and looked toward the floor.

"If you need time to think about this, I understand," I said.

"No, I want to connect with him. I miss him so much. But you know, he's dead, and I'm alive, and I really need to connect with someone here. I need love here, not a dead person loving me!"

"And I am sure he wants to help you with that. But we need to work through whatever messages Spirit is bringing you. You can't shut things out because you're sad," I said.

"I totally get it," she said. "I didn't mourn his death at all."

I now had to switch gears entirely. I needed to focus on connecting with a deceased person, which actually is an entirely different type of connection than a psychic reading. This stuff is so damned confusing sometimes. But I knew that the Spirit World is very rarely wrong, and when the Spirits show me something, or tell me to do something, I have to listen to their direction.

Richard put me in a scenario. In my mind, I was visualizing a car drive, and I could hear music in the background. As I listened carefully, I could make out that it was Donna Summer's "Last Dance." I verbalized to Caroline what I was seeing, and she immediately confirmed that I was seeing the moments before the fatal accident.

"You're seeing—our last—our last moments." I could tell she was sad and unsure of herself. She stammered a bit. "You see, I survived the car accident, and he didn't—that's where a lot of my guilt comes in," she confessed.

"I'm understanding that now," I said to her.

"I could have easily died too. I was in the hospital for six months after the accident. I had to have a lot of surgeries and stuff. It was terrible."

"Was 'Last Dance' actually playing when you guys got in the accident?"

She began crying profusely, and as her eyes watered and the tears trickled down her face, some of her makeup and eye shadow seeped down with it. I pushed the tissue box toward her, trying not to get too emotional myself.

"How do I move forward knowing that it could have been me that died and not him? There's a lot of survivor's guilt with me," she said through her tears.

"You see, a man isn't going to fix this. Being in a relationship is not going to just instantly heal what you are going through. You're still mourning. In fact, you haven't mourned at all with your fiancé dying."

"You're right. I haven't at all."

Richard showed me a heart on a silver chain. Caroline needed more validation. To really get into all of this with me, she needed to really get involved and take it all in.

"Do you have any connection to a piece of jewelry with a silver heart on it?" I asked.

"Yes, that was a piece of jewelry Richard gave me for our anniversary. I still have it," she said, more tears forming in her eyes. "This is getting intense. This is real."

"That's just his way of bringing up something that is very important to you and significant to your relationship to show you that he can really still understand and remember those experiences," I said.

She nodded as if she understood, but I wondered if she really did.

What began as a simple reading about this woman's love life—the typical questions that almost every thirty-something woman asks—turned into a healing reading about this woman's ability to overcome tremendous loss.

And then, as if things hadn't been strange enough, I could feel the light in the room shift. The lamp next to my reading chair flashed a bit. It even started to get cold in the room.

Richard hadn't just popped in for a visit. This was more than just a reading about being on the Other Side and missing him. There was a lot more going on here. There was a deeper message. I was about to find out why it was that Richard had practically forced his way into the reading room that day.

Richard showed me an image of a gun. A small handgun. Then he showed me a bedside table—white, cream colored, with brass handles on it. Damn it—what now?

I described what I was seeing.

"It doesn't ring a bell," she said quickly.

"Did he own a gun?" I asked.

"No," she said without emotion.

As an intuitive, I see a lot of people in my private practice. Women, men, old, young, all types of people. And you may call it psychic, intuitive, or just plain common sense, but I've developed an excellent lie detector. I knew for a fact that Caroline was withholding something. Just her reactions seemed incredibly strange. Here I was delivering her very concrete and specific messages from her loved ones, and I was seeing things she was relating to. Suddenly, I saw a gun in a bedside stand, and she had no reaction to this? I thought this to be very strange.

"Well, that's very strange because I am literally seeing a gun, and then I see this bedroom with all white and beige furniture," I said.

"No idea," she said again.

I decided to hold a space with her that was totally silent. We just sat there together. I wanted things to unfold naturally. We entered into a staring contest of sorts. I looked at her, waiting for her to confess what I knew we were getting at.

"Well, I own a gun," she finally said.

"Why do you have a gun in your bedroom?" I asked, in a tone that expressed how concerned I was.

"I don't know—it's stupid really—it's just really dumb," she said.

"Caroline, have you thought of suicide?" I asked, sitting up in my chair.

She paused for a moment. "Yes. I sometimes have."

"Caroline, I want you to get rid of that damned gun!" I blurted out.

"I think I can. I'm ready," she said.

"Well, I do too, because after we are done here, we're going to go to your house," I said.

Now normally, I keep strong boundaries with my clients. I believe it's my place to be as neutral as possible. But occasionally, I have to think outside the box, and I have to just act from my heart rather than my head. I wanted to make certain she was going to get rid of this gun, and I also wanted her to see that I wanted to be there for her in a way that nobody had ever been there for her before.

We finished up the reading. Although a few more validations came through, Richard had gotten through loud and clear to Caroline. And while Caroline had come hoping that I would tell her if she was going to meet her next boyfriend on JDate or Match.com, she had left the reading possibly saving her own life. See—and you wonder why I trust dead people more than living ones?

"Okay, let's go get that gun," I said.

"Now?" she asked.

"Yes, Caroline. NOW!"

On the subway ride to her apartment, we didn't talk much. It was 4:00 p.m., and luckily, I didn't have any clients scheduled after her (I had three as of last week but for "some reason" had decided to move them the week before). The subway trickled along, pushed forward, into the darkness searching for some light at the end of its tunnel. The A train trickled on, and we both were silent. I had a headache from everything that had just transpired.

Caroline turned to me. "I'm not ready for love, am I?" she asked curiously.

"We're all ready for love, Caroline. As human beings, we all want love. But sometimes we have to do work to prepare first. Guns in the trash first, boyfriends second." We both laughed at the craziness of it all. I was simply thankful that Spirit had somehow compelled her to come and visit me so that someone could give her a message and help her.

We walked into Caroline's one-bedroom Upper East Side apartment; it was dimly lit by one lamp in the kitchen. Caroline's close friend Margie met us at the apartment. I didn't want to be in a situation that would be uncomfortable, and I wanted someone who knew Caroline very well to accompany me. I had Caroline call her from my office and meet us there.

Margie was a thirty-something woman who had been Caroline's best friend all of her life. Margie and Caroline had attended Harvard together and been roommates since freshmen year. Margie was the only person that Caroline would see for a year after her fiancé had died, and that even included her family members.

"Where is the gun?" I asked.

"It's in the bedroom drawer—in the side table," she said.

"Is it loaded?" Margie asked.

"Yes, it is," Caroline whispered.

"Jesus Christ!" said Margie "A loaded gun?"

"I know, Margie, but I'm so sad."

"Caroline, I had no idea. You can always talk to me," Margie said to Caroline, running up to her and putting her hands on her shoulders.

We all went into the room together. I stood with Caroline by the bed, and she reached out to hold my hand. The room was so tense and dense with energy. We were all on edge and nervous. Margie walked toward the bedside stand and opened the drawer. I stood on my tippy toes to peek over and see what the drawer held in. There was the small black gun I had seen in my visions. It's funny to see things in real life that I see in my crazy psychic brain.

"Jesus Christ, Caroline," Margie said, as she turned back to look at Caroline and me. Caroline shook her head.

Margie grabbed the gun and immediately unloaded the bullets. We both winced as she did so—a very scary situation. For a moment I thought, *Am I really in a stranger's apartment with a cat, two strangers, and a gun? I mean, is this really my life?*

"Is that the only one of these that you have?" I asked Caroline, knowing intuitively that it was. She nodded her head to say yes. I breathed a sigh of relief.

With the gun unloaded, and our nerves a bit relaxed, we left her apartment and walked toward the Hudson River, with the gun in a plastic bag and the bullets in another bag. Fear still ran through me, and I did not feel calm. It was now almost 7 o'clock and getting dark out. Our plan was to throw the gun in the river. A ceremony. Caroline brought a picture of Richard with her so he could see it. Of course, we all knew that we didn't need a picture of Richard anywhere for him to see things.

As we climbed down the bank toward the river, I thought about what a complicated day this had been and how Spirit had used an opportunity for a reading that would seem to be so simple and basic to essentially stage an intervention.

A lot went on for Caroline that day. There were a lot of shifts in her mentality, and new ways of looking at problems were opened up. She had connected with her late fiancé, and she had finally dug into some wounds. We had also possibly, through this reading, saved her life.

"You ready?" I said, as I looked at Caroline, who held the unloaded gun in her hand.

"Very," she said.

"Now listen. You don't get to just throw the gun away, and that's it on this one. You have to promise me you're going to see a therapist after this," I said.

"I promise," she said and stuck out her pinky finger. We linked pinkies.

"Now throw that thing in the water!" I said.

She laughed, and tossed the gun like a boomerang, causing it to make a splash a few feet away.

We all felt relieved.

As we turned away from the river together, Caroline looked at me. I could see some happiness in her eyes, and her eyes seemed to be lighter.

"Thank you, Thomas—thank you."

"Don't thank me," I said. "Thank Richard."

The next month, Caroline and I met for a follow-up session. With the healing work done around her fiancé, she was now ready to meet a new love. Her guides ended up channeling a lot of information to her about what would be happening in her future love life, including that a man was coming into her life in the next six months.

Almost eighteen months later, I received a letter from Caroline. Well, it wasn't really a letter—it was an invitation to her wedding. Caroline met her soulmate about five months after her reading with me. As I had predicted, she met him through her friend Michelle, and he was married once before and had a child. Even though this wasn't what she had necessarily anticipated, she fell madly in love with the man because he was caring toward her and treated her wonderfully.

Life isn't what we expect, and even with the best-laid plans, things sometimes turn out completely in the opposite direction. When Caroline entered my office that first day, she didn't expect to hear from her fiancé Richard. And, likewise, when Caroline entered my office, I didn't expect to connect with dead people—I thought I was just going to read the cards around her love life. This was a surprise even for me. And when Caroline got in the car that fateful evening and caressed Richard's hand, as they talked about where to source the napkins for their upcoming wedding and how Richard's mother would *surely* be a nuisance during the wedding, she didn't expect Richard to take a corner too fast, hitting a tree and throwing himself 500 feet from the vehicle.

Every person who walks through my office doors has a story, and every deceased person around that person has a message. Caroline didn't come that day to learn about her love life. Even though she thought she was going to get psychic predictions, she got a reading from her late fiancé, which was much more meaningful. Until she heard from him, there was simply no way she could move on to even think or entertain a new love. Of course, a lot of this wasn't conscious, but that is how things become so blocked. And then, we turn a corner. We see inside ourselves. We have a moment of great insight. All becomes safe, sound, and clear.

These moments in readings and in my experiences with people are truly the closest things to a miracle I have experienced. Wayne Dyer says that miracles are in moments, and I believe that this is totally true. Sometimes people have a loved one come through who might say, "Well, okay, but what's the message?" But isn't that the message in and of itself? If the message is simply that our dead loved ones are around us, that they love us, and that love is a connection that defies the quantum physics of the Earth, well, isn't that message enough? I think that's a great message.

# CHAPTER 3

# TEACHING MOMMY

*"A happy family is but an earlier heaven."*
—George Bernard Shaw

"Let's play, Booger man!" screamed the young boy Spirit who appeared to me as I was shopping for toothpaste at the Duane Reade. He flashed me a smile of mischief. His hair was light blonde, thick and coarse, and his eyes were deep crystal blue. He wore a pair of denim jeans and a flannel shirt. He folded his arms and stuck out his tongue. His skin was a white porcelain hue, with rosy cheeks. By all accounts, he looked as though he was alive, except I knew he was dead. Nobody else in the store could see him except for me.

Dead people communicate in many ways. Sometimes they communicate through images or impressions, and I actually see things. These can be things I see externally or internally, in my psychic imagination. When the Spirits communicate verbally, it's much the same way. Sometimes they communicate through telepathic voices, and sometimes they communicate externally through voices that I hear like voices that you would hear if you were talking to a friend over a cup of coffee. Sometimes I see them as real as a person who is sitting next to me. In this case, the boy was speaking to me externally.

"Na Na Na Na Na—I'm dead. You can't catch me! You can't see me! You can't see me!" the boy continued, laughing, and then disappearing.

Even though the boy was dead, I recognized him. He had been appearing to me for the last couple of weeks. It was starting to become strange. Four or five times a day, he would appear and start laughing or teasing me. He had already made things in my apartment move in the middle of the night, and he was appearing in my dreams. The only problem was that I had no idea who he was, what he wanted, or how to get rid of him. I wanted to help him, but each time I asked if there was something I could do for him, he would just laugh and run away or say something mean. Sometimes younger Spirits are playful and like to tease me. I figured that this situation would all figure itself out in time.

I turned the corner to continue my shopping, going into the next aisle to look at some light bulbs. Several feet away, as I peered through bulbs, a wire tossed itself from the shelf onto the floor. I looked in disbelief. The boy Spirit appeared again.

"Blah blah blah, you're a ham, you're a cam, you're a slam slam slam!" he continued, screaming nonsense at me. As he did this, he moved toward some cans in the aisle and pushed one onto the floor. As it fell and hit the ground, he giggled loudly and shook his fists in the air. Even though I have seen this happen before, it always baffles me when Spirits are able to move things in the physical world.

He was so silly acting that he made me laugh. Even in the Spirit World, many people retain their personalities. Obviously, this boy had been funny and silly in life, and he was the same even in death. Still, I was unsure what he wanted to communicate.

"What do you want?" I asked. "I'm a medium—I can see you. Everyone else can't see you, but I can see you." I could tell he was not fully aware of what was going on by the way he was acting, and I wondered if he even knew that I could see him.

"You can?" asked the Spirit boy, turning around and looking behind him and in front of him, as if to see if he was on a stage or if other people were staring at him.

"If you can see me, what am I wearing?" quizzed the boy.

He might have been a new Spirit and didn't quite understand how all this worked just yet. Sometimes when Spirits first leave the Earth and travel to the other side, they don't realize that I can actually visualize them and see them. But after a bit of time, they start to realize that some living people can actually sense and feel them.

When I see deceased people, it can happen in many forms. Some people ask me, "Do you *actually* see them over there?" and the answer is yes and no—and mostly, it depends. The deceased people choose how they want to communicate and be seen to us. They can choose to come through in a way they wish to be remembered (younger, before they were sick, or when they lived in a certain place). They might also come through in a way that gives comfort to the people they want to communicate with or helps provide the most closure to the person I am trying to connect with. Often, they will just come through how they will be easily remembered.

Sometimes, I don't see the physical form of Spirits—and even when I do, it's just an illusion. It's just them showing me something so I can describe it to the person sitting there. In truth, they aren't in the physical form anymore, but they can take on the physical form for a brief period so we can recognize them and understand who they are.

"You're wearing a flannel shirt and jeans," I told him bluntly.

He stared at me, biting his lip. We both stared at each other for a moment.

"Wooooooooooooooooo!" he erupted after several moments and disappeared again. He startled me a bit with his loud scream.

I didn't make much of it and figured that if he had a message for me or someone else, he would probably seek me out again. Usually, though, when Spirits appear to me, they have a specific message for me. I see plenty of dead people all day, and I figured if this boy really had a message for me, he would find a way to communicate it to me so I could help him. In the back of my mind, I knew that I had to prepare myself for the fact that this boy might return to me with a specific message, and I would have to honor this and communicate it to whoever needed to hear it.

As I turned to go down the next aisle, there was the boy again. This time, he stood, hands crossed, in front of me.

"Look," I said to him, "if you aren't going to tell me what you need, I can't help you, and I'll need you to go and leave me alone. If you want help, you need to tell me what you need," I said sternly. I don't like being harassed by dead people.

We were silent for a moment as he took it all in.

"I need to talk to my Mommy. My name is Ralph," he said with a frown. Suddenly, he turned from a crazy dead boy who was stalking me to someone that I deeply cared about.

"I can help you if you need. Is your mom one of my clients?" I asked. Often times, Spirits visit me ahead of time if they know their loved ones are going to be seeing me.

"No," he replied timidly.

"Well, how am I going to help you if your Mom isn't one of my clients? Have I met her?"

"She's up front, Booger man!" screamed the boy.

"Up front?" I asked.

"She's up front, sneaky man; she's buying stuff!" the boy giggled and ran off down the aisle. When he got to the end, he looked down toward the cashier section and pointed.

"Mommy!" he exclaimed.

I walked down the aisle, approaching him. As I got halfway down the aisle, he disappeared. I got to the end of the aisle and looked toward the registers. A woman was standing there cashing out. She was dressed very casually in a ripped sweatshirt, heavy sweatpants, and her hair tossed in a bun. Her face seemed tired, with dark circles under her eyes. Gold jewelry hung around her neck. She was in her thirties, I would estimate, and the young boy was probably six or seven years old. However, Spirits come through in whatever way they think we will recognize them best, so sometimes the way we see them might be just the way they want us to remember them, and not the way they actually looked. So sometimes they might come through very young because they want to be remembered as young.

The whole thing was very nerve-wracking. My palms were sweating, and my forehead was sweating. Of course, I was nervous because this Spirit boy had been playing pranks on me all week. But I'm always nervous to approach strangers off the street and start giving them messages. I'm always worried this approach could backfire on me, or someone won't be into it or will be scared by what I have to tell them.

I gazed toward the woman cashing out at the register and quietly made my way to her. I watched her, and as I got closer, I could hear her talking to the cashier.

"No, I want the 100s. Marlboro Light 100s," she said, slamming down a pack of cigarettes onto the counter.

The man placed a pack of cigarettes on the counter in front of her and started ringing up her other items—Doritos, Junior Mints, ice cream, and Pepto-Bismol. I didn't really like her energy and vibe at all. She seemed hostile and bossy, and I was worried that if I said anything, she might snap at me. But I also know that the Spirit World doesn't really make mistakes, and if this dead boy was coming to connect with his mother, I had no choice except to deliver the message.

The woman took a double take at the cigarettes in front of her.

"Are you *deaf?*" she screamed. "I said I want 100s! The long ones! Are you deaf? I mean what the heck." She blew out a deep breath, showing her exasperation, turning to look at the people in line behind her for support.

The cashier frowned and rolled his eyes, grabbing a pack of cigarettes from behind him.

As my attention drifted away from her talking to the cashier, I noticed the young Spirit had appeared again. This time, he stood behind her. He frowned as he looked at her, and then he looked at me.

Mentally, I communicated to him. "I'll talk to her. I'm going to talk to her." I can communicate with Spirits telepathically or verbally (like I would speak to a regular person). It really doesn't make any difference which way I communicate, as they hear and experience the message the same way. But in this situation, I definitely didn't want to speak out loud and have her see me talking to a Spirit.

The boy nodded. From the cashier's face, I could sense the relief he was feeling by her leaving the counter and his store. As she turned, he rolled his eyes in frustration.

The woman moved away from the counter with her bags. I could tell by the way she was quickly walking that I would have only a brief opportunity to connect with her before she turned and left.

"Ma'am?" I said as she moved from the counter.

She turned around immediately. "Don't call me ma'am. That's for old people. My name is Debbie. What do you want?"

"Well, nice to meet you, Debbie. I'm Thomas," I said, a bit taken back by her abrupt reply.

"Are you the manager? Because I want to explain about that loser behind the register," she said, interrupting my train of thought.

"No, I am not. I don't work here. Look, I'm sorry; I don't want to bother you or scare you, but I have a message for you," I said.

"A message?" she asked, raising her voice a bit, in a tone that seemed utterly confused.

I explained to her what I did, and the experiences I had had over the last couple of minutes. I even described what her son looked like and that he was visiting us now in the store. I knew that the only way she would listen to me was if I gave her some specific information that only her son would know.

"So, you're like a psychic?" she asked, taking a step back as she said it.

"Yes, that's one way you could say it," I said, in a tone that sounded ashamed and unsure of myself.

"I don't believe in stuff like this at all. Those people just guess," she said and moved toward the door.

I'm always surprised when people say they don't believe in this type of stuff. I guess I think it is surprising only because even if you don't believe in something, if something comes through so specific for you, wouldn't you believe in it? I don't understand how you would really have a choice. Often times, I guess, it's a fearful thing. In other words, they are scared of the unknown and don't want to believe in it. I thought it was particularly strange because I had already given Debbie some specific messages. For example, I had said to her that I felt her son around her, without any prompting from her. Maybe the situation would have been different if I had said that I saw her father or mother or grandparents, as she was an older woman, and maybe they could have passed, but I specifically said her son.

"Ma'am, I think you should listen to me, as I really do have a message for you, and I don't think your son would be visiting us if he didn't have a special message for you," I said.

"Look, I don't know how you know I had a son that died, who told you that, or what's going on, or if you think this is funny, but I absolutely do not want to hear anything you have to say. You have a lot of nerve even coming up to me. Seriously—get lost before I call the police!" she screamed at me.

By now, the cashier and two other people in the store were staring at us. I was completely embarrassed and mortified at the entire situation. I was also dumbfounded—from both sides. Why would someone not want to hear about her son? I had specifically mentioned I was connecting with her deceased son.

Normally, I would never push myself on someone. I always respect people's boundaries. But I also know that almost every time a Spirit visits, it's for a specific reason. And if this boy visited me, I knew he had a special reason. I was going to be damned if I let this boy down.

I knew that she didn't believe. I knew when she was saying that, she truly meant it. And I knew that unless I said something that really blew her away, she wouldn't listen to anything I was saying. And I knew that her son would never come through to me so strongly unless she needed to hear from him and he was here to help her.

As I had that thought, I had a simultaneous image of a yo-yo come to my head. The boy Spirit standing next to me showed me a yo-yo too. I could see the yo-yo in his hand. It was clear plastic with a hint of yellow to it and a Donald Duck logo on the side. All of this transpired within split seconds.

"He has the yo-yo," I exclaimed. "The one with the Donald Duck on it."

She stopped walking toward the door and stood still, her back to me. She turned and looked at me.

She then dropped her bags. Tears began to fill her eyes. "I really miss him," she said. I had connected, and I knew her life was about to shift in a really major way. She reached out to hug me. Stuff was about to get real.

That was the moment of change. This is the defining moment of every reading and every intuitive message that I give. When something becomes real and tangible for someone. All of the "He's okay," "She misses you," "You'll see them again," "Your grandmother has roses," and "Your mother wanted to be closer to you" messages sound great and feel wonderful—but to get to that point, I need that clear validation. That one specific thing that nobody could possibly know. That magical secret that allows for healing to really bloom and begin. The psychic seed of change.

"His name is—" she started, before I cut her off, because the boy had also provided me his name just seconds before.

"Ralph. He told me," I said.

She nodded. It was really him. "You're not pulling my leg, are you?"

"Nope. I have better things to do," I smiled. I wanted to give her as much evidence as possible.

"I'm sorry I yelled at you. That wasn't right of me. I'm sorry, and I am ready to hear what you have to say if you'll let me hear it. I've just been through so much," she said.

"It's totally okay. And if it's okay with you, I'd like to try to connect with him and see why he is coming through so strongly," I confessed to her.

"Okay."

I paused for a moment and then started to connect. "Is it his birthday?" Suddenly, he was showing me a birthday cake in my mind's eye. I could see the candles burning brightly and lighting up the blue and white frosting.

"Today is his birthday," she said, a tear forming in her eye. She was clearly very moved by the message and was opening up to what I was saying.

"I am seeing a cake with blue and white frosting—it looks like it has an image of Cookie Monster on the top of it."

"Oh my God," she exclaimed. "That's the last cake we had together. That was his birthday cake the year he died."

From there, she listened and received. I started to tell her about how her son had passed away and about his funeral. The boy was channeling messages to show her it was really him, and she was really accepting of those validations. Often times, people need to hear validations before they can truly start to receive messages of guidance or comfort. They need to really know it is their relative or their significant other coming through. If I start by just giving messages without describing who or what the person looked like or the role this person had in their lives, it's too confusing and it doesn't help the people really take in the message.

"He's concerned about the family. He's concerned about the dynamics of the family."

"That makes sense. Things aren't really going well there. Does he say if they are going to get better at all?" she said as she wiped her tears away.

I felt so much sadness coming from her, and I saw images of all sorts of dramatic situations in her family—fights, glass being broken, screaming, and sadness.

I closed my eyes and focused on what the boy Spirit wanted me to communicate.

"He's trying to help you with the family situation," I said to her. "He knows you and the family are struggling."

"We are," she confessed. "Since he passed away, it's never been the same."

"What do you mean?" I asked.

"We just haven't recovered. There's so much sadness and pain with us all. We're not over this. We don't know how to be. We are totally stuck. We all mourn in many different ways."

"Who is Danielle?" I asked. I heard that name in my head. Although Debbie and I were talking, the boy was still connecting with me and giving me information.

"Danielle—that's his sister," she said, a bit confused and dazed. I think she was still surprised how much information was coming through.

"He knows about her. Was she born after he crossed over?" I asked.

"Yes, she was born only like six months ago. My psychiatrist told me I should have another child to help me with the loss of losing Ralph," she whispered.

When people pass away, it's very confusing for us who remain on Earth. We wonder if our loved ones are aware of what goes on here after they pass away.

"He's in a good place. You need to focus on things you can deal with. You need to focus on the things you can actually change. Especially your beautiful new daughter."

She nodded, sobbing, wiping her face with a tissue. "I needed to hear that."

"You know, I owe you an apology," she said.

"You don't owe me anything. I totally get it," I said.

"I had this one experience and it was really bad. It was a long time ago, but it freaked me out. The woman couldn't connect with my son and then she told me that he was stuck on the Other Side, and she needed thousands of dollars to help him cross over," she confessed.

"I get it," I said. The fear I had been sensing before had been real. She was truly scared of connecting.

"It helps me to know my little boy is in a place where he is peaceful, and that he can still come around with me."

"He definitely can. He loves you very much," I told her.

Debbie and I parted ways that day, and I never saw her again. I knew the closure that Ralph had given her through me had been immeasurable. Even from the ten minutes we spoke, I could see that she became a totally different person—calmer, more relaxed, less tension in her body.

Spirits of every age and every type can come through to guide their loved ones from beyond. Even if Spirits have been gone for fifty years or if they were very young when they passed, part of their contract with their soul family on

Earth is that they continue to guide us when we need it. Even though this boy was very young when he passed, the knowledge that he had about his family's struggles and how to overcome them transcended space and time.

# CHAPTER 4

# "YOUNG HEARTS RUN FREE"

*"Coincidence is God's way of remaining anonymous."*
—Albert Einstein

One thing I have learned in doing all of these readings with people is that the dead people are a lot more intelligent than the living people. When people transition to the Other Side, they leave their living bodies here on the Earth, and they become more spiritually aware, more insightful, and more full of love. This happens almost instantly. They have this way of being all-knowing and fully engaged in our lives. Often, they aren't psychic or always aware of what will happen in the future, but instead, they are almost like a great friend who knows everything and is wise and smart. Having a dead person watching over you is like having a really smart best friend who always seems to know what to tell you to do in any situation. Many times, the deceased people plan and orchestrate a series of events in order to allow us to learn certain lessons or hear certain messages. Sometimes we don't even realize they are doing this until days or weeks later when the pieces start to come together. I've had many moments in my life when I've thought, *Damn it! Why didn't I listen to that dead person?*

At a large audience-style reading in Michigan, I was channeling messages from deceased loved ones. In total, there were about 200 people in the audience, and I was standing toward the front of the room describing Spirits that were starting to visit the room, in the hopes of reaching members of their living family. Although in most of my work, I do private, one-on-one readings, I also do larger events where I have an audience of people come and receive messages. Although everyone does not receive a message in these larger group readings, they are extremely popular because they are financially sensible (tickets are only $50) and you get to bear witness to what can often be an incredible and uplifting experience. Even those who don't get a message can be deeply moved and shifted by the experience.

The evening progressed as it normally would. I delivered readings to those in the audience when I felt a particular Spirit come through.

"I'm hearing the name Douglas or Doug, and I am seeing a young male in the Spirit World."

The Spirit was young, new, and I could tell had only recently transitioned. He was very eager to communicate.

Usually, when I start to get information from the other side, people in the audience are a little timid at first. Nobody wants to really claim something because the information that comes through is increasingly specific, but at the beginning, it's fairly quiet. If I throw out just a name, nobody is really likely to raise his or her hand.

This time a woman timidly raised her hand. "I know the name Douglas. That's my son who died."

The woman who raised her hand looked very put together. She had short hair, very styled, blonde with highlights. She was maybe in her mid-sixties. She wore a white pantsuit. Her jewelry was restrained—gold earrings and a gold bracelet. She looked strong and confident. Her face was carefully painted in light makeup, with a red color around her lips and quiet brown shadow.

"Douglas is your son?" I asked to verify.

"Yes. He passed away," she said.

Next to her, a woman began to stir. You could tell she was having a reaction to the entire situation. She wore a dark gray sweatsuit with a paint stain on the shoulder. She was a bit overweight, with glasses, and a mole on the side of her nose. Her zippered hoodie sweatshirt had a dinosaur on it. She wore white sneakers. Her hair seemed unkempt and strangely parted. She was nervous as she sat there. The two women were a complete juxtaposition.

"Is she connected to you?" I asked the woman in the sweats, pointing to the more stylish woman.

"Nope," said the first woman, looking toward the other.

"Well, actually, my son died and his name is Douglas, too," said the woman in the sweatpants. With that, the second, more timid Spirit stepped toward me and waved at me.

Both women looked at each other stunned.

This is a common experience. The Spirit World will sometimes place people next to each other because they want to somehow connect the people who are there. It's very strange—it's as if their energy connects to one another. On other occasions, I have had three suicides sitting together, four people with dead husbands who didn't know each other sitting together, and one time, I had a small group reading for twelve people (none of them knew each other and all had just randomly purchased a ticket) and every single one of them had just lost their mother in the last two months to cancer. The Spirit World likes to orchestrate grief support groups. It's their way of showing us that healing and transition have a common thread.

"This happens a lot," I explained to the audience. "Sometimes the Spirit World puts people together who might have shared experiences. It's a very common thing."

Both women nodded.

"Let me see if I can actually discern who is coming through or what is going on," I said to them, and closed my eyes to tune back into the Spirit World.

I tried to tune in more. I saw a calendar. It spun to the month of May, and then the 4th was circled. "I am seeing the date of May 4th," I reported.

Both women gasped.

"My son died on May 4th," the blonde woman said.

"Mine did too!" said the other woman.

They both looked at one another. The woman with the dark hair reached out and grabbed the hand of the woman sitting next to her—the other woman with the dead son. For a moment, they both looked into each other's eyes.

"This is just too weird," one of them said.

To be honest, I couldn't argue with them here. I was beginning to think that this *was* getting a little strange. A name, the same death date, the same type of relationship to the person.

"Let me see here," I blurted out. I wanted to bring together the space and the energy between all of us. In a way, the whole thing seemed strange that they would be sitting next to each other.

I asked for another message. I needed something else. We needed to know which Spirit was coming through at the moment.

"I saw a car accident, so which son died in the car crash?" I asked.

"Mine did," said the woman in the sweatpants.

"As did mine," said the other woman who was more nicely dressed.

At the strangeness of it all, we all laughed, as did other audience members in the room.

I decided to change my method of questioning the Spirits. It was clear they were both coming through. This could not be some coincidence. This was a planned synchronicity experience. I needed to know why this had happened. What was the lesson we were all supposed to learn here?

Suddenly, flashes of the lives of these women came before me. I saw the woman with the blonde hair and felt the success and happiness in her life. I felt the way she overcame her son's death. I saw flashes and images of how she had started a charity and how she had honored her son. I saw how she had written a book about his death and how she had helped many people to overcome the loss of their own children by sharing her personal message. Then I saw flashes of the woman with the dark hair. I saw the sadness and how her life had become totally frozen. I realized that the reason these two women had come together was to show them how different their lives had evolved and the different meanings they had taken from virtually the same experience.

"There's a lot of strange stuff going on here," I said. "We need to dig into this further."

Both of the women nodded.

"What's going on here is that we're supposed to all learn a lesson here—from these two women. We're all supposed to learn what happens here with us is all varying forms of the same spiritual lessons. We are all spiritual beings having spiritual lessons in various forms."

I received a steady download of information—I was seeing names, places, dates, and information that was all totally relevant to their individual lives.

The message of this experience was to embrace the fact that it's truly not the events and circumstances that happen to us that really matter. In other words, even though something happens to us and it seems really significant, it doesn't really matter. Instead, what matters is what we do with that lesson and how we let it impact and affect our experience.

In all the chaos of this experience—losing a child in such a tragic way—there were two messages here from the Spirit World. One was the message that there truly was something here beyond what we were seeing or feeling. There was an organizing principle to it all. There was chaos and sensible organization where there had been utter disorganization and confusion. There was also a clear understanding that part of the message here was about the fact that things were different for both of these women.

The two women had very similar experiences. Both had sons pass away. Both were similar ages. Both of the deceased sons had left behind people who cared about them. Both women had not had the opportunity to say good-bye to their beloved sons. In a way, their situations were totally identical. However, what the women did with the experiences was totally different. One woman had decided to take on the experience head-on: she had decided to start a charity in honor of her son, help get legislation passed in her state for heftier fines for the prosecution of hits and runs. She was fearless, fabulous, and strong. She even changed professions and became a psychotherapist to help grieving parents who lost children in tragic ways. She didn't want to leave this world without making sure her son's legacy would never be forgotten. The other woman had a different reaction to things. When her son died, her entire life shut down. She became miserable, she got a divorce, she lost her job, she gained weight. She had cancer twice. Her whole life had been turned upside down, and she had stayed in a position of sadness and of anger. She was unreachable.

But in the end it wasn't what happened to these women that really mattered. It mattered more what happened next— what they did with the experiences and how they let those experiences shift their lives.

"Are our sons together?" the woman in the sweatpants asked.

"Yes, they are friends on the Other Side," I said. "Since their experiences were so similar, they have befriended each other. They are helping each other carrying out certain missions and goals."

As the women left the event, I could see a new connection would be formed. They gathered at the door talking to each other, and I could see the sense of recognition and compassion within their eyes. They knew each other's stories. Although these women hadn't known each other previously, I knew that they had been led here by their sons. I knew that their sons had even placed them next to each other so that there would be tremendous connection and compassion. This is why I say that the Spirit World is always in charge of every decision we make in the world.

"I felt my son here today, and I miss him. It's nice to know that he's found a friend, and that they have so much in common," said Margaret, the woman in the sweatpants.

"Yes, and that they can share a birthday cake. We even found out that both our boys loved the same ice cream cake from Carvel."

People say that life has no coincidences, and that everything we go through and experience has a purpose and has a meaning. And while I'm not sure I believe that 100 percent, what I do believe is that certain experiences are so profound and rich that they can't be explained by anything else besides the wisdom of God, the angels, and the Other Side. Imagine having a helicopter view of the world—of seeing everything from up above, and being able to navigate where there were roadblocks, traffic jams, or fires. That's how it is in Heaven.

# CHAPTER 5

# HOCKEY GOAL

"A friend is someone who knows all about you and still loves you."

—Elbert Hubbard

During my private readings, I usually allow only one person to come and sit with me at a time. Sometimes, however, I will allow an additional person to sit in on a reading for emotional support, but during the reading, I strictly focus on the person I am reading and connecting with. In that way, I can make sure that everything that comes through in that moment applies to only the person sitting there.

Two summers ago, I went to the Jersey Shore for a couple of weeks to visit. My plan was to relax at the beach and do some readings.

The day before I left on the trip, I got an email through my website. The subject line said "Your upcoming trip to the Jersey Shore." I didn't recognize the sender's name, and I assumed that the message might likely be from someone wanting to have a reading done while I was on my trip. Unfortunately, I was booked up way in advance, and there were no slots left.

The full email read:

Dear Thomas:
Last year, my husband Paul lost his best friend Christopher. The entire situation was very tragic, as they were closer than brothers. My husband has completely changed his whole mentality about life, our relationship, and family since his death. He is in a huge state of depression. He does believe in an afterlife, but he's having a terrible time connecting or feeling his friend around him at all. Is there any way we can meet in New Jersey and have a reading?
Best, Leslie.

I started to write a letter back to Leslie explaining I was booked in advance, and encouraged her to seek me out the next time I was down in the Jersey Shore. As I typed the letter, a Spirit appeared to me in the mirror next to my computer.

"Stop!" the Spirit exclaimed loudly.

"Don't write that. I need to speak to my friend," said the Spirit, audibly, like a person would be talking to me if he was alive and in the room. This Spirit was having a full-on conversation with me.

I saw a man standing next to me, as clear as day. I could tell he was dead because his image was floating. He wasn't standing straight, he was wobbling all over the place, and he occasionally disappeared entirely and then reappeared somewhere else in the room.

The man was in his early forties, with a dark beard, long hair, and dark brown eyes. He wore a flannel shirt over a t-shirt, jeans, and dark lumber boots. He looked strong, rugged, and he was very tall. He looked like a lumberjack. His face was stern. A cold air seeped over me, as I sat there, a bit shocked, and a bit in awe that this bossy, domineering Spirit was trying to tell me what to do and what not to do.

"That's my best friend's wife writing you, and I need to connect with them," he said to me, channeling the thought in my head.

I never argue with a dead person. When people die, they truly act from a place of guidance and helpfulness. They do not act from a place of the ego. They don't care about what living people think or what people want or what people say. They only care about delivering the most healing, powerful, moving messages.

I knew that this Spirit had visited me for a reason. And if he told me that he needed to reach his friend, I knew that there was a specific reason. Spirits don't try to control or dictate or ruin things. They really just want to be there out of emotional support and love. Unlike living people who act for their own needs, wants, and desires, those in the Spirit World act only in a way to guide us and let us achieve our highest good.

Trusting the guidance of my deceased acquaintance who had come to visit, I called Leslie and confirmed her for Sunday evening. Even though I knew I needed a day off, I also knew that the universe always provides opportunities, and I knew the universe would not put me in a predicament. Somehow, this would all work out—I just wondered how.

�֊

I greeted Paul and Leslie that Sunday evening at the one-bedroom apartment that I always rent when I go to the shore. It's just a simple place, very simply decorated, casual. I've rented it for three years in a row, and I normally spend two weeks down at the shore every summer. I have a big following down there, so I will do a slew of readings, relax at the beach, see some friends, and make a little vacation/work trip out of my time there.

Paul and Leslie were a striking, beautiful couple. They were young, vibrant, probably both in their late thirties. They just *looked* amazing together—like one of those couples that you instantly understand how and why they are together. She had long, brown hair, beautiful curls, with a well-groomed appearance. She was tall and very thin. She wore black jeans, with a white top, and she had her hair pulled back in a pony-tail. He was equally striking. He had a short, dark cropped hair and a little cleft in his chin. They were both athletic and well built. Leslie had glowing, radiant skin that had a subtle shine to it. I could tell from the way they walked into my apartment together that they were very close and very loving to one another. They were holding hands, and together, matched perfectly, as if they had come to life out of a painting.

"It's our first time doing something like this, but we both believe in it," Leslie said, with Paul nodding his head to affirm.

"Well, welcome," I offered, as I shuffled things around on the table in front of me.

"When I connect with the Spirit World, I start to get images, impressions, feelings, and sensations. I will describe those to you, and then you should start to get a sense of who it is I am connecting with. I am going to try to focus on your friend, but someone else might come through too." I described my process to them in detail.

"Is it okay if I cry?" Leslie asked.

"Sure," I said. "Sometimes I even cry!" We all laughed together.

Every time I begin a psychic reading, I feel a little bit different. I've never begun a reading feeling the exact same way as another time. Sometimes I feel anxious, worried that no information is going to come through. Other times, I worry that the information will be too disorganized and that nothing will make sense, or I won't be able to keep track of it all.

In this case, I knew from the situation with the email that I received from them that there was a male in Spirit, and I knew also from the email that it was this man's best friend. But I also wanted to allow the session to be what it is. I didn't want to make any assumptions, and I knew from the way things work that sometimes the person you would expect to come doesn't show up. Immediately, I sensed a male around me. I could see dark hair and dark eyes. I was being shown glimpses of photographs in my memory, and I recognized that some of the photographs actually included the people sitting in front of me.

I described one of the photographs in detail, even describing the clothes and some of the colors I was seeing.

"Those are some of the last pictures that we took with my friend who died," said Paul. "We were just looking at them before we came here," he said as he glanced at his wife.

"That's your friend's way of validating that when you were looking through those images, he was actually standing with you," I said.

Paul started breaking down crying. As a man, even a sensitive one, I know it can be difficult to cry in front of someone else, especially another man. I didn't want to comfort him and make him think that I was belittling him or patronizing him. I let him cry and pushed a box of tissues across the glass table toward him.

"I'm also seeing a Bruin's jersey—a Boston's Bruins jersey," I said.

"That's amazing—we buried him with that," Paul said. "It was his favorite jersey."

Validation after validation came through, so we knew that the person we thought was coming through was definitely coming through. Although this is always the fun part of the reading—the surprising details that the Spirit conveys that blow everyone away—there always needs to be a deeper message, too. There needs to be a take-home message so that we know why it is this person is seeking out the sitter to communicate.

So, as the reading continued, Christopher started to open up. Paul and Christopher weren't just friends—they were best friends and almost like brothers. Christopher had a very troubled life. He was abandoned by his parents when he was young, and he was always depressed and sad. He started drinking at a young age—first, socially, and then it grew from there. First, he would drink a couple of drinks, and then he'd drink to get drunk. Then, he started to experiment with drugs and smoking marijuana. Paul watched out for Christopher and basically took him under his wing. Family holidays, graduations, dinner parties—Christopher was very much a part of the family and always around. He was the best man at his friend's wedding. He was always connected to Paul. Christopher described much of this in the reading with Paul. Even though Paul already knew this, of course, it was nice validation to hear his friend describe the dynamics of the relationship.

Christopher was always "the bad guy." He was always the troublemaker, always chasing girls, always causing problems. Paul was very different. He was a good student and star athlete; he had a full scholarship to college. In high school, they both played football. Paul was the star quarterback, scoring more touchdowns in his senior year than any other quarterback in the history of the school. Christopher was a scrappy linebacker and didn't do much on the team. He was often late to practices, and in his junior year, he almost got kicked off the team because of his poor grades and allegations that he had brought booze to the campus.

As time went on, Paul and Christopher became very different people. Paul got married, started a family, and started to build his life. For Christopher, his life became more about drinking, partying, and medicating his problems. He wanted to avoid anything related to dealing with his issues. Christopher and Paul stayed in touch, but their friendship wasn't the same. It all felt forced. A few times, Paul (at the heeding of Leslie) confronted Christopher about his drinking. He would tell Christopher that he was going to cut him off if he didn't stop drinking, not speak to him anymore, and end their friendship. But somehow, it always came back to their becoming close again. They would work things out. It was never clear how, but they did. Because they had such a brotherly friendship, Paul couldn't stay mad at Christopher for very long.

Paul had deep issues around his friend's death. He had not achieved closure with it because he truly felt that Christopher's death was his responsibility in some way. If only he had intervened in Christopher's drinking. If only he had called Christopher that night when he said he would.

The truth is, during our existence on Earth, we are complete spiritual beings that are primarily having a brief human experience. We are here to learn valuable lessons around humility, immortality, vulnerability, and resilience. Although we continue to have other incarnations in other dimensions, the Earth is a place where we come to learn specific lessons that often deal with our soul's journey toward self-acceptance and unconditional love for humanity.

This is why I think it's remarkably inaccurate when people say, "Wow, the Earth really sucks" or "Life just sucks, and that's it." I don't believe that at all. I believe the Earth is a perfect playground.

"Are you wearing his chain?" I asked Paul.

"Yes, I am wearing his chain," he said. His wife gasped a bit. Paul pulled out a chain from underneath his shirt and confirmed that it was Christopher's favorite necklace. It was a silver chain with a small cross on it. He held it as he looked up at me.

Sometimes I tell clients pieces of information, and I'm not even clear how I get the information. It comes to me so quickly and all of a sudden that it's just an idea in my head, like an idea that anyone else would have, like "Oh, I should go and file something my drawer" or "I should fold my laundry after I get home from the gym." These are moments of claircognizance, in which clear thoughts come into my head and I can immediately feel that they are accurate pieces of psychic information.

An idea popped into my head and I said, "Were you supposed to be with Christopher the day he died?"

Paul fully understood what I was talking about when I mentioned this.

"Yes, absolutely. We were supposed to see each other that day, but we didn't because he was in one of his depressive states, and we just ended up not connecting that day. Sometimes Christopher would get very depressed and totally shut the world out."

"You're holding Christopher back. You're holding him back from going to the next level in his spiritual development," I said. It was Christopher who was now telling me this. His friend Paul was so focused on his death and harbored so much guilt, resentment, and fear that Christopher was actually having a hard time transitioning to the Other Side.

"How am I doing that?" Paul asked.

"You're so scared of losing him and so scared of his death that you're holding him back. You need to let him go. He's on the Other Side now, and he has things to work on over there. You can let him go," I said.

"He was my best friend. I just miss him," Paul said. "But I know what you mean."

"And he still can be your best friend. Even though you can no longer physically touch him or physically be with him, you can still communicate with him. They hear your thoughts and actions. So it's still a real connection; it might just be a little different because you don't see or touch the person like you do when there is a physical connection.

"I understand all of that—you know, for a guy, I'm pretty open to this stuff. I just never feel him around. It's like he died and forgot about me."

This is a common question people ask me: if the Spirits are so around, why don't I feel them? The answer is that truly "feeling someone" can take on many different forms. Spirits might show you that they are around in very subtle, quiet ways—it might not always be the most obvious message.

"Are you playing hockey tomorrow?" I asked. I had suddenly been shown an image of a hockey game, and I felt that it was a message I was supposed to deliver to my client.

"Yes—I am playing tomorrow, in my league, and Christopher played a lot of hockey with me in his lifetime," said Paul.

"You're going to score a goal tomorrow—the winning goal, and the last goal of the game—and Christopher is going to help you with it," I said, as the scene played out in my head.

"So that will be like him guiding me?" asked Paul, sounding a bit confused.

"Exactly!" I said.

The next day, I was spending time with a close friend of mine, Karen, a peppy blonde girl. We hadn't seen each other in a few months, and we were catching up over coffees. I was focusing on our conversation, and to be honest, I had totally forgotten about the reading I had given Paul the previous day. I give many readings, and sometimes it's hard to keep track of everything. I also often ask to not hold personal information because, really, it's not my information to hold, so I don't want to retain it. If I did, I would probably be an emotional basket case.

A text popped up on my phone as Karen and I were sharing stories and catching up.

"Just scored the winning goal . . . the goalie was Christopher. Sign or what?"

I smiled. Suddenly, Christopher appeared next to me.

"See—I told you to read him," he said. He winked and disappeared.

I laughed.

"What are you laughing about?" my friend asked.

"Nothing—life is just funny," I said.

The reading for Paul was all about validation. He believed his friend was still around him. He trusted that his friend was all around him. He wanted his friend to be all around him. But this reading really showed him that this was the case. There was so much validation and closure here.

Sometimes the smallest, most insignificant thing can turn into the most powerful, thought-provoking message. A lot of healing transpired that day for Paul and a lot of healing even went beyond the reading room.

❧

Every day, start by connecting with the higher source and deity of the universe. If we can do this, our lives can truly shift. Seeing the universe in this way allows us to have stronger connections with each other and, ultimately, ourselves.

On Earth, our lives are filled with illusions. We have to create certain illusions on the physical plane in order to survive here. For example, even the concept of time is an illusion created only to make our lives here easier to comprehend.

There is great clarity here—we see the choices we made and don't judge ourselves.

I try to not get too emotional when I am working, and in fact, I ask for guidance from the Spirits around me to not allow me to cry or shed tears. I do this because I am here to provide a service to people who are truly in need of hearing from their loved ones. For me to cry or have emotional reactions to things can dampen the process a bit and make it clouded. I have compassion for my clients, as compassion can heal, but empathy at a high level, all the time, can actually be negative and hurt us.

Every molecule, part, component, and element in us is formed in the heavens and in the divine presence of our angels and our creator—and so if you don't believe in miracles, it might be a good time to remember that you actually are one. Your mere existence, and that you came into this universe, is a blissful, spiritual miracle.

# CHAPTER 6

# TONY

"The weak can never forgive. Forgiveness is the attribute of the strong."

—Mahatma Gandhi

Sometimes I do large group readings where 200 to 300 people gather in an auditorium space and I deliver messages from the deceased for two to three hours. When I do this, I start to describe Spirits that I am picking up on until someone in the audience claims the Spirit. These are basically ways to reach large numbers of people and have a great amount of healing go on in a short amount of time. Because of the work I do, it's not possible for everyone to have a personal experience with me with a private reading. These group readings are tremendously healing and powerful experiences that can really move and shift consciousness.

During one event in Florida, I was channeling all sorts of messages. Dead animals, dead children, dead grandmothers. A tremendous amount of healing was going on, and the night was truly powerful and moving for many of the people in the audience. Even people who did not get a message were clearly moved by some of the profound healing messages going on. The messages were very simple and clear. Nothing too shocking or out of the ordinary.

As I moved toward my next connection for the night, a young male Spirit appeared to me. I could visualize him, but only very faintly. He seemed disheveled—sad and a little out of sorts. I felt a tremendous amount of sadness and discomfort from him. I almost felt that he was confused or ambivalent about actually coming through and contacting someone. I felt he didn't want to be there. I could make out that he was maybe in his twenties; he seemed to have darker hair, longer; and I could see his arms a bit; and I could see tattoos. I could see him outside my mind, as if he was standing in the room with us, but his image was hazy and formless.

"Are you okay?" I asked him.

"I am doing okay. I've come to apologize," he said back to me. He then showed me a gun.

"There's a man coming through with a gun, and I am sensing a lot of regret from him. He is between twenty and thirty years old," I told the audience.

A few people in the audience whispered to one another. I could see people scanning their memories to see if they knew anyone that would fit these context clues. Nobody offered anything, and I felt that I needed more information from the Spirit before I could truly go further with this.

"My name is Tony," the Spirit told me.

"His name is Tony," I revealed to the audience members.

A woman in the front row, who had already seemed quite eager, raised her hand and exclaimed, "My grandfather's brother-in-law was Tony, and he had a gun collection." Immediately, I knew this was wrong. This person had passed much more recently.

"I think this is someone more recent than a great uncle like that," I said.

Next, I saw a flash of Dorchester, Massachusetts, a place that I remembered from childhood. I paused for a moment to think about things. I also had a friend from Dorchester named Tony. I wondered if this was my imagination or an actual psychic message. I decided to stick with what I was getting and describe exactly what Spirit was showing me.

"I just saw a flash of Dorchester, and I got the name of Tony."

It was strange because I was doing this seminar in Boca Raton, Florida—not in Massachusetts. So, I wouldn't expect Dorchester to be a really common place that many people in southern Florida would know about or reference.

"Does anyone connect with Dorchester?" I asked.

Silence again.

"Massachusetts? Dorchester, Massachusetts," I pushed.

I turned to the Spirit next to me. He shrugged. "She's sitting in the back," he communicated.

I moved toward the back, taking the cordless microphone with me. I pointed to the last two rows.

"Does anyone connect with a Tony back here? Dorchester?"

This woman looked at me and made eye contact and then looked away. She was older—in her sixties—dark hair, well kept, short. She was dressed in a white sweater and khaki pants, and seemed nervous. Her blue eyes scanned the room as I continued to stand next to her row. In her hands, I noticed her holding a silver rosary. Nobody sitting near her seemed to be related to her, so I wondered if she had come alone. The name Greg flashed in my head, and so I offered that, too.

"There's a Greg connection."

With that, she gasped and put her hand up to her mouth and started crying. She looked directly at me.

"Are you connecting with this information?" I asked her.

"Sort of," she said. She seemed startled.

"It's important if you think something is for you that we figure out if it is or not—I don't want to ruin the flow of the evening," I reminded her.

"Well, Greg was my son. And he died of a gun shot. And he died in Dorchester. And Tony . . ." she trailed off.

A few people in front of her turned around.

"Tony has come to apologize," I said. Immediately, I heard the words "I'm sorry" over and over in my head, like a repeating chime on a cell phone.

She yelped a bit and then began to cry.

"That's the name of the man who killed my son. He's dead, too," she whispered.

The room sort of fell silent. Wow. Never had that happened before. I thought to myself, *Damn, dude, you have some guts coming through from killing someone.* Sometimes I even shock myself, and that was one of those sometimes. This was definitely a first to have someone who killed another person come through to apologize to the family. I almost didn't know what to say. So many questions flashed through my mind. The first thing I thought was, *How is this person communicating from the Other Side (Heaven) if he committed a murder?*

One of the things that I have come to understand from the Spirit World is that the concepts of Heaven and Hell are not necessarily accurate descriptions of what happens on the Other Side. If we do bad things here—murder people, abuse people, steal from others—on the Other Side, we are held accountable for that behavior in some form. But instead of being punished or made to shovel coal in a ditch, we actually must experience the spiritual lessons that provide us with teaching to overcome these imperfections and spiritually grow from these imperfections in our characters and these mistakes.

I felt as though I needed to give her an option. I couldn't force her to connect with the man who had killed her son. "Do you want to connect with that person?"

"Yes, I do. It's actually who I want to speak with," she said, standing up to take the microphone. I could feel she was ready.

"Every time I go to a medium, my son comes through, and I know that he is okay. But I need to hear from Tony—I need to know why he ended my son's life," she added.

Immediately, Tony started to channel information to me. With her blessing and permission, he was ready to speak to her.

"I keep hearing that this man murdered your son—but I also feel that they were close friends." I said this because I had seen, in my mind's eye, a handshake, which is my symbol for friendship or close friends.

"They were," the woman said, as she put her hands on her face. "They were best friends."

Suddenly, I had an image of an argument in my head. I heard loud shouting.

*"I can't believe you would do this to me. How could you sleep with my girlfriend?"* I heard playing in my head. It was almost as if I was tuning into a movie. I shook my head a bit and relayed what I was hearing.

"Yes, that's true," the woman said. "My son and him had a major fight over my son's girlfriend. The whole situation was just really bad. And my son didn't even do anything wrong. It was all just in Tony's head. He had a lot of problems as a kid, but I was like a second mother to him. I basically raised him."

I immediately got a message in my mind that this boy had committed suicide shortly after the death of this woman's son. I didn't see anything and I wasn't shown or feeling anything—I just suddenly had a sense of clear knowingness.

"He took his own life," I blurted out, surprised by my frankness. I didn't want to intimidate her and say too many accurate things all at once—it could make her uncomfortable.

"Yes, that's true," she said. "Everything overwhelmed him, and he ended up ending his own life." She put her head down. "It's just a very unfortunate situation," she said, as she shook her head and looked at the ground.

The whole room was silent for a moment.

"He was a close friend of my sons. I asked him to come through today. I needed to understand this. We're all just so sad about it. His mother and I have been very close. Does he know that?"

I mentally asked him and he said he did. For validation, he offered that he had been around them last week when they were together at the memorial run. She confirmed that was true; the woman had done a memorial walk for her son, and the other mother had come to support her.

"It's just all so tied in with everything. The whole situation is tragic from both sides. There are no winners here. But I came to understand," she said.

We were quiet for a moment. I felt there was more.

"Why did he do this? Why did he kill my son?"

Questions like these are incredibly loaded and incredibly difficult for me to answer. The reason is that, in reality, answers to these questions can help, but only in certain ways. For example, even every answer that a Spirit can come up with won't bring him or her back to Earth. Even a connection that is so validating and so strong—it won't bring back that person. I always tell people that even the best medium cannot replace your connection with your loved one here on Earth. That's why when you are on Earth, it's important to cherish and value every second that you have with people that you care about. No reading can change that type of connection. That's why a lot of people come for psychic or medium readings. They come to understand and to hear things that they might have known, but were too frightened to embrace or really take in.

It is truly shocking how, in some instances, the most bizarre, uncanny experiences can call themselves forward to manifest opportunities for growth, evolution, and change. We can't control really what situations manifest in our lives. We can't decide what obstacles or challenges God gives us. As some have said, we are merely actors here, we are given roles, and we must do our best job at acting in them.

Closure for us can come in so many ways. Sometimes we need to hear from people we love; sometimes we need to hear from people that we're surprised would even come through. What we must always understand is that on the Other Side, Spirits do not have egos. They don't come through for attention or their own personal agendas—they come through in order to helps us on Earth and provide us with the highest amount of healing and forgiveness that is possible.

Suddenly, I felt another person with Tony. A second Spirit appeared. This time, it was a brown-haired boy, muscular, wearing a white t-shirt and jeans. He had a big smile on his face and was laughing. I felt so much happiness from him. "I'm her son," he said as he gave his friend a high five. They stood together.

"He's with your son over there," I said. I described the boy who stood with Tony, and the woman validated that is what her son looked like.

"I wanted to see if they were together," she confessed. "I'm surprised to see that they are after my son was killed by him, but in a way, it makes sense. They were so damn close."

It might seem strange that the man who killed another man would be in the same place on the Other Side, never mind actually being together. However, even though one man had killed the other, they were still very much connected. This was all part of the same experience, and many of the same emotions were running through both of these women at this reading. This was tragedy, but somehow the people on the Other Side had to make sense of it. To spend time with the person who murdered you—well, this is the true definition of forgiveness, I guess.

And that is truly what a reading does: it makes sense out of tragedy. Its organizes the experience and reshapes it. It puts knowledge where there is ignorance, clarity where there is confusion, and peace where there is discomfort. The healing power of a reading like this is that it shows the true capacity for the human spirit (not always the human being) to truly transcend emotions like anger, rage, and animosity, and move toward higher-level emotions like forgiveness, peace, and harmony. A reading can give great capacity to understand a complicated situation and see it at its raw, emotional core. It can detoxify the experience.

Many times in a reading, we actually know exactly what the answers are to our very pressing questions. It's just that we don't want to admit that we know the truth, and refuse to trust our own inner instincts.

At the end of the evening, the woman from the reading approached me and gave me a hug. She thanked me for the messages from Tony and from her son.

As she walked out the door, I had an image of Tony and Greg sitting together, arm wrestling, and enjoying one another's company.

Forgiveness is the most healing emotion. The woman who got the reading clearly had forgiven Tony, so much so that she had done the unthinkable: come to face the man who had killed her own son. Her son had also forgiven Tony, as evidenced by their being together.

# CHAPTER 7

# THE TWO DADS

"There are more things in heaven and earth, Horatio,
Than are dreamt of in your philosophy."
—William Shakespeare

The two men appeared, and I immediately recognized they were father figures. Visually, I always see what Spirits looked like in the physical plane, but I also see energies around them. I see a lot about their personalities, their characteristics, and how they were as people. I also get a sense of the traits that they had.

Immediately, I was shown the image of a gun, and when asked if this made sense, the couple sitting across the table from me agreed that it did. The names flashed before me: "Bruce and Tom." Unlike the shadows, these messages came through clearly, written on the ethereal blackboard, spelled out right in front of my consciousness.

Jennifer and Josef, who had entered as skeptics, now sat mesmerized, confirming what I was seeing.

Earlier that week Jennifer had called, demanding a session.

"I need an appointment as soon as you can fit me in," a piercing voice demanded from the other side of the phone. Before I had a chance to answer, she asked, "Is it going to be a long wait?"

It would be. I had a one-month waiting list at the time. As a psychic, I can do about six one-hour readings in the span of a day before I am completely drained, burned out, and exhausted, making information that comes through somewhat unreliable. There are only so many hours in a day that you can talk to the living, much less the dead. They both can zap your energy quicker than a ten-mile run on a summer day.

I felt badly about declining a client whose marriage seemed dependent on a timely reading, but I thought it was unfair to cancel other clients who had been waiting an entire month just to accommodate this somewhat haughty woman. "I don't have anything now, but let me take down your number," I told her. "If someone cancels, I'll call and you let you know. If it's meant to be, it will be."

Surprisingly, she seemed okay with this. "I'll pray for a cancelation," she said.

Those guiding us on the Other Side can be incredibly direct. Often they seem to guide us, making sure we get the information we need at the correct time we need it. That was the case here. The next day, I received an uncharacteristically high number of cancellations: four. And Jennifer took the first available time slot.

As soon as I encountered Jennifer and Josef in my waiting room, I knew the reading was going to be very moving and sad. I almost wanted to cry. This isn't a normal reaction, but if I sense that a reading will be particularly intense, I sometimes begin receiving sensations immediately before the reading.

Now the couple looked at me anxiously, expecting me to reveal their future. . . .

I receive information through all of my "clairs." These are *clairvoyance* (mental visions), *clairsentience* (where I feel things, like you would feel emotions), and *claircognizance* (where I simply "know," much like you just "know" that hot water burns). So I start to build a case. I ask the Spirits for names and very specific information, like a street where someone lived, birthdays, special places, or memories. I ask to be shown places, such as where the Spirits had lived or things they did while on Earth, so the people across from me can hear the validation of the deceased being around them. I feel that names are crucial because if I can learn a name, I can really grasp the essence of the person to whom I am talking. I don't like to play the initials game; you're coming to a psychic, not playing Scrabble. An initial is not sufficiently specific or authentic.

"I am seeing a pair of shoes. Your father, Bruce . . . ," I said pointing to the woman, ". . . is telling me that he bought you your first pair of shoes. The old tap shoes, the white ones you have by your bed."

She gasped. "I did have white tap shoes." And yes, she did fondly remember buying them with her father, and yes, they were right above her daughter's bed.

"Yes, but he said they were above your bed, so he was wrong," Josef insisted, looking at me with a mild frown.

"Your father is here, too," I pushed past his skepticism. "He wants to tell you he met Mick on the other side; he found Mick?"

I watched Josef's eyes get watery. His face crumbled, and his voice turned small and sad. His cheeks became puffy. As he turned away from me, he explained that Mick had been his childhood dog that passed away in a fire many years before his father's death. As he talked, I saw the tragic scene of a fire burning in a pink house and a dog yelping and whimpering. The image and sounds became so real that they shook my body, and my spine tingled. I twitched a bit. Then I saw blood and guns. I described this to the couple, who began to weep.

"It makes sense that you would see that," Jennifer said, validating my visions but still holding back; she didn't say why it made sense at all.

When I do a reading, it can be nerve-wracking, because I am literally seeing events in a puzzle. Pieces start coming together. Nothing is ever linear. What I am shown evolves as more and more pieces of the story fall into place.

"I hear yelling and screaming. It's really, really loud, and I feel drunk or high. I feel almost sick to my stomach." A sense of nausea filled me, as dizzying screaming shook my head. My head was pounding, and my ears even rung with the lasting impressions of my intoxicated visions.

They both nodded in rapt attention, eyes wide with disbelief.

"Is there a message they want us to know?" Jennifer said, wiping her tears away with a tissue. Although Josef had started to appear emotional earlier, this was the first time the woman had started to show any sort of emotional reaction to the images I described. Still, I felt she was trying to make the whole process cold and scientific. She didn't want images and emotions and screaming—she wanted messages.

Messages are hard to deliver. When people say "messages," they usually want to know the answer to a "why." Why has this person come through? The response can frustrate clients, usually because the message is just too simple: the Spirit simply wants to say hello. That's usually not enough "connection" for dabblers. Other times, it's more complicated. Maybe the Spirit wants to talk about something that's going on in the client's life, something unresolved from the past that needs fixing.

*"They want you to know that even though they can't be at the wedding, they approve of the marriage. They are shaking hands, and though I feel they had difficulties here on Earth, together on the Other Side these men are friends. They don't disapprove of your wedding. They will send you a rainbow on your wedding day. They will be there."*

Her father's words flowed *through* me now, instead of just *to* me. He had taken over my mind and body. When I said the words, it was as if I was listening to someone else speaking; I didn't even quite understand them.

Up to this point, I really had no confirmation that anything I was saying was even making any sense, besides a few minor details, which is not unusual. Many times during readings, people are very quiet. They don't want to share a lot of information, and they want to keep a poker face in a misguided attempt to "trip me up."

"What you're saying is making a lot of sense," Jennifer finally admitted, her face stern, but hands shaking. "Our fathers did business together, but our families never knew each other. Three years ago, our fathers got into a huge fight at a bar, and my father shot his father. He was so distraught he checked into a hotel and shot himself. We met through our fathers' deaths, and mourned together and fell in love. We are here to make sure we have their blessing to get married," she burst out crying just as the last word poured from her mouth. She reached for another tissue.

It takes a lot to surprise a psychic, but this story absolutely stunned me. I was truly flabbergasted. I replayed her confusing and strange words in my head: "Did business together . . . my father shot his father . . . shot himself . . . met through our fathers' deaths." I turned the phrases over in my head. I needed to find a way to get these words to sink in, but they confused me. My heart was pounding rapidly. Part of me understood so deeply. As a psychic, I wanted to believe—and know—that two fathers, whose hate for each other in life ended up killing them, were now putting the past behind them in the name of true love. As one family had died in bloodshed, another family would be born of this blood. But there was also the pragmatics of it all, and the side of me that was absolutely stunned that someone could sleep next to and share his life with someone who had the same DNA as the murderer of his father.

"Oh," I said.

"We came here to make sure we could get married and that our fathers gave us their blessing. You are saying that we are okay to get married?" she whispered at me, her voice going up like she was skeptical and not believing.

"I am not saying anything. They are speaking through me," I corrected her. I was only the messenger, not the sender. I enforced my neutrality: don't put this on me, babe. At that moment, we traded places. The nonbelievers had become the believers; the sage devotee had taken a step back; this was getting all too real.

"We want them to be together," Josef's father said.

"We approve," said Jennifer's father. "We love them."

"They love you. They both approve," I translated to Jennifer.

"What does it mean that they love us?" Jennifer asked. I didn't know if I would even be able to get a clear answer.

Jennifer's father stepped forward.

*"The way that we show our love on the Other Side is unconditional. On the Other Side, we see the true essence of our loved ones on Earth. We love without expecting anything in return, we accept our loved ones even with their faults and flaws--and that's the purest type of love there is."*

I repeated the words to Jennifer, word for word. She squeezed her fiancé's hand.

We sat there for another ten minutes. Jennifer wanted to know about her father's transition. Josef seemed shaken by the whole thing and didn't say much, but occasionally, when I said something that seemed to strike a chord, he'd nod his head a bit in disbelief and stare at the floor, saying, "Wow, this is crazy."

We wrapped up the session with a quick prayer. Jennifer wanted to say a prayer for her father and father-in-law. This wasn't a common request, but I decided to honor it. Together, we said an "Our Father" and ended the session. As we said the last words together, I began to notice the Spirits of their fathers slip away. The room was somehow more empty, and I could breathe—really breathe—again. My clients gathered themselves and made their way for the door. I waited for them at the exit. As Josef walked out, he thrust out his hand to shake my own. Jennifer passed by nodding, almost in a whisper, "Thanks. Thanks."

Before they left, I felt their energy and mood significantly lighten. Previously, they were dripping nervousness and tension. However, after the reading, their energy felt calm and serene. Jennifer could embark on married life without wondering if her father was suffering for his terrible deeds. Josef was relieved that despite marrying the woman whose father had killed his own, his father was, indeed, at peace with his decision to marry her. I breathed out a sigh. Onward and upward.

As the days progressed, I thought about Jennifer and Josef. Their story stuck with me. Everyone who sat in the room that day—dead or alive—had learned an important lesson and also made a rare connection. For the fathers, they could be given closure for a terrible situation that has brought their families through a living hell and back. For the couple, they could continue on their journey in good conscience and no longer live in fear or worry. And I learned about the cycles and synchronicity of life, and how all things strangely come together and how we can't avoid or deny it. Such is the case in these situations that are truly too deep and complex for our conscious minds; we inform them with our own significance and our own interpretations of their greater purpose, and just end up accepting it because we don't have an answer key. There *is* no big reveal. We cannot, and never will, find out if we are right or wrong. So it's just easier to assume that we're right.

I wondered about strange questions in the days after Jennifer and Josef left. They had met through the deaths of their fathers, and admitted they would never have met had it not been for the tragedy. I wondered how they reconciled that very fact. Did they ever ask themselves: "If I could have my father back to sacrifice our love, would I do it?" I wondered: *If God said, "Hold on. Time out. This is weird; do you want a redo?" would he or she take it?* Luckily, this was a choice neither had to make; the Other Side decided to spare them. The Other Side knows best, I guess. Maybe we don't need to know all the answers, all the intricacies, or the very DNA of every metaphysical event we are blessed with experiencing. In a way, it feels better *not* to know why this had to happen, but rather, to just embrace—and accept—that it *had* happened that way. Sometimes it's really easier to just believe. But even I—the spiritual one, the medium, the psychic—had serious doubts. I wondered, especially in this case, *Does everything have some great purpose? Was the plan really that two men would die to bring together two lovers?* It just seemed over the top. So my faith—my belief—wavered.

On Saturday after their reading, I arose early to go for a run in Central Park. Small drops of dew beaded up on the bench seat. The sun shone brightly above me. I thought about the couple and what a gorgeous day it was for a wedding, and I felt happy for them. I attempted a psychic impression of how their big day was progressing. I felt blissful and joyous. As I ran, the quick beat of my heart matched my rapid steps.

After a session, it's not unusual for clients to write me and follow up. So I wasn't surprised when, a week later, I found a note from Jennifer in my Gmail:

Dear Thomas,

We so enjoyed meeting with you last week. We were amazed with the details that came through, and were happy to know that our fathers approve of our union. I will admit, I was disappointed that I saw no rainbows or fireworks on the day of our wedding. I just assumed you might have misheard or misinterpreted something. However, the next night, as I thumbed through photographs of Dad, I came upon a rainbow patch wedged between the photographs. I have no idea where it came from. It was really bizarre because my mother, who is still in mourning, goes through those pictures at least once a week, and says she has never seen it before, and has no idea where it came from either! Everything you said was great, but honestly, this was the moment I fully believed.

Thanks Dad.
Best Always,
Jennifer

# CHAPTER 8

# MATERNAL LOVE

"All that I am, or hope to be, I owe to my angel mother."
—Abraham Lincoln

Before I read someone during a private session, I always meditate on the person's energy to see if I feel anything prior to his sitting with me. It helps me to attune myself so that when I begin to read the person, I am completely ready to connect. It's like doing a light warm-up before doing a workout. As I tuned in on my client—Phil Ginsberg—the face of a woman appeared in my head. I immediately knew that this was his mother and that she would be the main person I would be connected with during the reading. "This is a reading about letting go and forgiveness," the female Spirit said.

The door opened from my office to my waiting room for my last appointment of the evening. I was a bit tired but ready to have my last appointment for the day and start a three-day weekend. Sitting there, tapping his foot, was a young man with dark hair, probably in his early thirties. He had light blue eyes and heavy, thick eyebrows. He was dressed business casual—dark navy suit, white shirt, no tie. His face was tan, with dark, chiseled features. His jawline was strong and defined. He looked like a business professional—someone who would likely be a real estate broker or banker.

Phil sat quietly on the couch as I explained to him my process for connecting. I told him that we'd begin by my connecting with whatever I saw or felt around him. I told him I would describe everything to him, and he could validate if things made sense or not.

"Sounds good," Phil said, shaking his head. "I've done this before with other people."

As I began the session, the woman's face reappeared—the same face I had seen in my vision. I also saw the rest of her body. She wore a nurse's outfit—white skirt, white hat, and a white shirt.

Immediately, I went to work knowing I had to connect him with someone. "Do you know anyone who passed away that would be a nurse? Or work in the medical field?" I asked.

The man's eyes opened up a bit and he stared at me. "Yes, my mother was a nurse."

Immediately, I felt pain in my hips. I felt a shooting, sharp pain. I screamed out "ow" as I sat with him. Often, Spirits will communicate with me by putting actual physical sensations in my body or emotional sensations. In both instances, this is called *clairsentience,* or clear feeling.

"I am feeling pain in my hips," I communicated, my eyes still closed.

"Yes, well, my mother died from basically a fall—she died by falling and hurting her hip, and then some other things happened." His voice changed, and he sounded nervous and a bit uncomfortable. He started to tear up a bit.

The Spirit of the man's mother communicated another feeling—a feeling that I only get in a very specific way. I get this heavy feeling under my eyes, and I start to see dark circles in my frame of vision. I get a pounding deep in my chest, and then I get a pressure deep in my temples. I get a shortness of breath, too. It's like this intense, deep feeling. My own body shakes and vibrates. It feels really weird.

"Your mother is telling me she was murdered actually—but she doesn't want you to think of it that way," I said.

He smiled faintly. Then, a tear fell from his eye.

"Well . . . ," he paused for a moment. "My sister . . . ." He trailed off and began to sob.

Immediately, I heard the name Marcy.

"Do you know anyone named Marcy?" I asked him, my eyes still closed.

"Yes, that's my sister."

As I experienced the name Marcy, I got a sense of depression and sadness. My head was dizzy, and I felt pain in my head. I felt depressed, anxious, and sad. I also got a clear feeling that I was somehow out of my body; I almost felt like I was high or drunk. My heart started to race.

As an empath, I experience people's energy when I am given someone's name. I have a way of being able to connect to the energy and feelings associated with that person. From there, I can sense how she is as a person, if she should be trusted, and what type of person she is, and what types of experiences she has here. Empathy is a very powerful, lucid emotional experience.

"Did your sister do drugs?" I asked.

"She used to be a drug addict," he said. "She's rehabilitated now."

As if watching a movie playing in my head, I saw a scene in front of me. I heard screaming in my head. I couldn't make out the individual words, but I could tell that this was a fight between two people, and I could hear two different voices, both females. Images and pictures flashed in my head very quickly, changing and rotating, and spinning around. Then I saw a woman fall.

"Did your sister push your mother?"

"Something like that," the man whispered, his voice sounding a bit quiet and shocked. "It's all very sad."

The Spirit of the woman in the nurse outfit stepped forward and told me she wanted to tell her son that she knew she would have died anyway.

"Is she okay?" he asked.

"Your mother is saying that she feels she would have died anyway. Was she sick?" I asked.

Phil nodded. "She had terminal cancer—she only had a few months left to live, if that. Then she got into a scuffle with my sister, and my sister pushed her and she fell and died." He began to cry a bit.

"She is saying she's happy you didn't prosecute your sister. She said that she was dying anyway. She only had a little time left. In a way, she died to save your sister's life—and she said that is the way you have tried to understand it and think about it."

Phil began sobbing again. I could tell from his deep breathing and his deep sobs that he had not cried like this in a long time. He was releasing tension, anxiety, and pain. His entire aura began to shift, and even his neck started to look more relaxed, and his shoulders relaxed a bit. He hung his head a bit low.

"I've been waiting six years to hear that," he said.

Phil explained that after his mother had passed away from injuries during the altercation, his brother, Jeff, wanted the sister prosecuted and put in jail. On the other hand, Phil felt she was an addict and severely disturbed, and that while he was sad about his mother's death and truly angry that his sister had acted in this way, putting her in jail would not solve the problem and not help her get treatment. He didn't want to lose another member of his family; he had already lost one.

"Mom always worried about Marcy. She always wanted her to heal," Phil said.

As it turned out, heal she did. Instead of sending Marcy to jail for manslaughter, Phil asked the prosecutor to recommend some form of addiction counseling and intensive treatment. The judge ended up putting Marcy in court-mandated, in-patient, intensive drug programs. Marcy healed completely from her major addictions. In fact, she healed so much that a year later, she fought in the courts to get back partial custody of her only child, whom she hadn't seen in ten years. She went back to college, finished her degree, and ended up getting a social work degree to help other people with addictions. Today on the speaking circuit, where she delivers lectures to college campuses nationwide, she talks about her life story and the challenges and obstacles she faced.

"In a way, Mom gave her life up to let my sister live hers," Phil said. A tear rolled down his cheek.

I could sense from the woman how she was in a tremendous amount of peace. Around her form, I could see a white light shining. She also showed me a dove, which is my sign for "I am at peace."

"You need to leave here knowing that there's nothing you could have done to prevent this, and nothing that you did wrong. She wants you to stop beating yourself up here."

He nodded. "I feel I can leave here knowing that my mother is at peace, and that she's not mad at me for not punishing my sister. I feel like I can maybe get through the years ahead and try to put this issue behind me. It's given me some closure."

Life is full of circumstances that can be painful, troubling, or traumatic. Whether it be a death of a loved one, a family feud, or a financial crisis, we all face situations that test our emotional and psychological endurance. Sometimes we are even tested by particular people in our lives who might hurt or injure us—sometimes even people that we love very much. But what the spirit world teaches us is that whenever we are hurt by someone, we should always work towards forgiveness. And while it can't always be immediate, if we can get there in time, we are all the better for it.

# CHAPTER 9

# THERE'S CHOCOLATE AND CHAMPAGNE IN HEAVEN

"Everybody wants to go to Heaven, but nobody wants to die."

—Peter Tosh

"I just don't like when you get in these bitchy moods," my friend Hannah said to me as I finished my dinner and got up from the table.

"I'm not in a bitchy mood, Hannah. I just don't feel like going all the way down to the Financial District to a party for someone I don't even know. It's 60 degrees and beautiful out. I kind of feel like being outside. I worked all day. I'm tired."

She was quiet. I could tell she was silently calculating in her head.

"There will be a lot of nice people there—cute guys, fun people. Plus after, we can grab a drink, just the two of us. I never see you anymore."

"You've seen me three nights this week," I laughed.

A lot of psychics hate parties and big events, but I'm not one of them. A lot of psychics are very sensitive and empathic, and we can pick up a lot of what's going on. It can make us sick, tired, irritable, cranky—and it can even cause health issues. However, I am really good at protecting myself and my space and setting clear boundaries with the Spirit World. In fact, I love to socialize. For some reason, when I'm not working, I still want to be around people. I get lonely easily—but not very often—because I usually have either dead people or living people to keep me comforted.

The only reason I dislike parties is the standard party questions that everyone asks about everyone's life—but in my situation, they are particularly annoying and redundant. For example, when I tell people I am a psychic, medium, or see dead people, they immediately want to know if anyone is around them or if there are any messages for them. They want to know how I first knew I had this ability, where it comes from, and if it scares me. Normally, I don't mind all the questions—but today, I just wasn't in the mood to go. I could sense in Hannah's voice a deep disappointment. I knew that if I didn't go, she would not go alone, and because she was newly single and trying to meet people, I wanted to support her in any way I could.

"Fine, I will go," I told my friend. "What time should I be ready?"

"Eight," she said.

When we arrived at the party, we saw a typical New York scene—a lot of people we both knew casually, a few close friends, and one or two people we didn't particularly care for. Like any party, the plan was to maneuver around, make introductions, and avoid those we didn't feel like seeing. After about thirty minutes, I was starting to get hungry, so I made my way over to the snack table and mingled with folks over snacks like olives, bruschetta, cheese, and wine. As I scooped up a bit of olives and cheese, I made eye contact with a woman who was cutting from a block of Mozzarella cheese and grabbing some crackers for her plate. Her husband motioned to some of the wheat crackers.

She smiled at me. "Great party," she said. "Indeed," I replied.

"Who did you come here with?" she asked me.

"Just a friend. We know the host. Old friends. You know how it is. I'm Thomas, by the way."

"I'm Joan, and that's my husband, Mark," she said, pointing to a man standing next to the mantle, biting into a quesadilla.

Sometimes you see a couple, and you just know they belong together. These two looked like they belonged together. They looked like the perfect fit. He had a strong jawbone, dark hair, and full eyes. He wore a white button-down shirt and khaki pants. He was thin framed but strong, and I could tell he really took care of his body. Her look was also striking—she wore a black dress and had red nails. She looked sharp. They appeared to be in their forties, but young looking. They were affectionate with each other throughout the night, and I could tell there was a lot of shared affection and attraction between the two of them. There was a feeling of closeness for sure.

After I finished grabbing some snacks, I made my way over to the couple, and we all started talking together. Something about Mark and Joan drew me in, and I was immediately interested in hearing what they had to say. She was super cool and very spiritually open, and we were talking about her many travels, their young kids, and how she had come into her own with her spirituality. She had never really been spiritual, but after her father died, she suddenly opened up to the idea of a universe beyond the one we live in.

"So what do you do?" she asked, sipping her wine and finishing her crackers.

Usually, I hate to answer this question at parties; I'll deflect it by saying that I have my own business or that I work with people in some consulting or counseling. To say that I am a psychic medium at a party with strangers is the equivalent of opening up Pandora's box.

"Oh, wow—I'm totally into that sort of thing. I once had a woman who read my cards in college. I'd go and see her frequently. I think she died though," Joan said. People always feel the need to tell me if they believe in what I do, what they think about what I do, or if they have ever seen a psychic before if they meet me at a party.

"So are you more of a psychic or a medium?" she asked.

"My focus is mostly on the medium side of my work—you know, connecting with dead people, but I do both and I like both."

"My father was not a spiritual man at all; in fact, he was a big atheist. But he promised me before he died that if there was life after death, he'd find a way to communicate," she told me, as we sipped on our glasses of sangria.

As she described her experience, her husband scowled and rolled his eyes. At one point, as she was talking about her connection with her father during a dream in which he had visited her, he laughed at her and softly whispered under his breath, "Oh, this is crazy," and walked away.

As he walked away, she looked at him and then looked back at me and laughed. "He doesn't believe in any of this stuff. He thinks it's nuts."

"A lot of guys are skeptical," I confirmed with a nod.

"It's sad though because he's not gotten over his mother's death. I wish he would open up to something like this. It might help him."

"I bet when he's ready he will. For some people, it just takes them a long time."

As I said this, I felt this painful, tightening sensation in my chest. I almost was having trouble breathing. It was kind of shocking to me how strong I felt this, and I was wondering if something was wrong with my body.

"She died of a heart attack last year, and he never got to say good-bye," she chimed in, taking another sip from her wine.

I wondered if the sensation in my body was really my feeling the Spirit of this stranger's late mother pass through me. He returned to our conversation, carrying a plate filled with appetizers—some celery sticks with a heavy cream dressing, a pot sticker, and some folded-up meat. He started munching on the snacks loudly.

As he chewed, I heard in my head, "Chew with your mouth closed, Mark!" in a scratchy, raspy voice that sounded like the voice of a woman who would have smoked. I knew immediately the voice was coming from a Spirit.

His wife started to change topics, and asked me about my outfit. I was wearing a loud red blazer, and she complemented the design of the jacket. "I love bright colors; they really show off in a room." She giggled a bit. The man's loud chomping continued.

"If your mother was here, she'd kill you right now with that chomping. Can't you just hear her? Evelyn had such a loud, piercing voice."

The voice I had heard in my head only a few seconds prior repeated in my head. Mentally, I made a note to myself and said a quick protection prayer. In a protection prayer, I mentally and spiritually call on my angels to protect and watch over me . "If this is truly this man's mother trying to communicate with me, give me one more piece of information."

In my mind's eye, I saw lights flickering—bulbs of a lamp blinking on and off. I wondered what it meant. I couldn't get the thought out of my head. I assumed it probably meant something related to this situation.

"Mark's just not into this type of stuff. It scares him. Doesn't it, sweetheart?" she said putting her hand on his cheek and gently rubbing it. She turned back and winked at me.

"It doesn't scare me. Alligators scare me. Murderers on the loose scare me. Horror films scare me. Crazy people talking about how Spirits roam the Earth and angels with wings on cards—that just makes me laugh," Mark said.

With that, the lights flickered all around us. Two lights on either side of the mantle we were standing next to blinked several times. The couple next to us spun around to look at the lights too, and a couple of men standing next to us turned and noticed also.

"Uh oh—there's your mother," Joan said. "She always flashes lights when her Spirit is around," she said, leaning into me.

"Will you stop it, Joan?" he pleaded and took a step away from her.

"I see your mother around you," I blurted out.

The woman paused before placing the last carrot from her plate into her mouth. She looked at her husband and looked me, closely examining the eye connection, likely gauging her husband's reactions.

"Oh, this should be good," she said, munching on the carrot.

"Oh, really? What does she look like?" he said, nonplussed by my revelation, looking at the tray of appetizers a waiter was carrying around.

"I'm not seeing her visually, like you see normal people."

"How convenient," he smirked and rolled his eyes to his wife.

She scowled at him and raised her eyebrows.

"I'm just getting the name Martina too."

He shrugged.

"Mark, your grandmother was Martina," Joan said.

"Isn't everyone's?" he said.

"Mark, stop it. Listen to him!" Joan said.

"This is ridiculous."

I knew we were at a defining moment. I needed to hit something really good. I needed to say something that could only come from his mother. It couldn't be her name, it couldn't be a random date, it couldn't be something too general. I had to hit home with this guy. His mother needed to come through with something clear and concise. *Give me something, Evelyn, give me something,* I mentally begged. I knew she was here—but I needed to convince him. I wasn't here to convince anyone of anything. But I did want this for him. I wanted him to have that validation experience.

"She can't believe Joyce came to the funeral," I blurted out, and held my breath waiting for a reaction. I honestly didn't even realize I was speaking. It wasn't until a second after I opened my mouth that I realized I had said something.

As I looked at Mark, something in his face changed. The color immediately shifted. I could see he was nervous but also welcomed the contact a bit. His mouth moved, and he licked his lips. He seemed startled.

"And what an ugly blouse she had on," I added. Again, it was like I was speaking, but I had no conscious thought.

He burst out laughing. "That's Mom," he said with recognition, tilting his head and raising his eyebrow, clearly expressing some disbelief. His face turned red, and a tear formed in his eye. I could see he was very moved.

"Oh my God," his wife said.

I didn't know what this message meant, but it obviously meant something. I didn't need to know what it meant.

This wasn't for me. It was for him. It's moments like these that I realize how, being a psychic medium, I have the ability to sometimes change someone's life entirely—and in a fairly short amount of time. The impact that this man's mother potentially had on him by coming through to him could permanently shift his entire conscious mind.

"Her friend Joyce came to her funeral. They were best friends, and they had this big falling out about two years before Mom died and never spoke again. And she did come to the funeral. We all were talking about how if Mom was there, she would have made fun of her blouse because it was horrible looking," he said, validating everything.

I could see, as he said these things, some of his skepticism was checking in. He looked at his wife for a moment.

"Did you tell him anything?" he asked.

"Of course not, you crazy person," she laughed.

"Wow, this is amazing—everything you said was correct," Mark said.

Now, it's not that I'm surprised when I get something right. I think it's a little preposterous when you see a psychic score a "hit" on a TV segment, and he seems more shocked than the guest. I'm always surprised by that—I mean, don't you do this for a living? Why are you shocked? But still, the quickness with which the man's mother reached me shocked me.

"Is she doing okay over there?" he asked, a tear forming in his eye.

"She is. She just said, 'There's chocolate and champagne in Heaven.'"

"My mother ate chocolate and champagne every night of her life after dinner for as long as I can remember," he said slowly, a smile on his face. "They have that over there?"

"They can have anything they want over there. Heaven is a personal paradise, so there aren't limits to what's over there. It's a state of mind as much as it is a place. Heaven is a place where everything is perfection, and everything is based truly in peace and love," I said.

I gave the man a few more messages, but really the woman just wanted him to know she was around him, how much she missed him, and that she was doing okay. She hadn't had the chance to say good-bye to him. The messages were profoundly comforting to him.

"That's amazing," he replied. He reached out for a hug and we embraced.

We all stood there in disbelief. Though I had witnessed this all before many times, it was still truly moving to witness a total skeptic become a total believer. The man was truly moved. I could feel his entire demeanor change. He seemed relaxed, less anxious, and calm. He was even breathing differently. He kept taking deep breaths in and out.

The party started to wind down, and my friend Hannah circled back to me.

"That was a boring party," she laughed. "How was it for you? I never saw you the whole time."

"I liked the party. It was fun. I ended up reading someone."

"Of course, you did," she laughed and rolled her eyes.

As I left the party, I realized why Spirit had sent me there. It wasn't for the conversation, the loud music, the cold-but-should-be-hot appetizers, or the long bathroom line. It wasn't for my friend I went with, either. It was for that man. Spirit needed me to go there so I could connect with this man.

"The food was good at that party. Did you eat?" I asked, as we buckled our seatbelts to pull out of the parking space.

"Just some chocolate and champagne," Hannah said. I smirked. I'm sure this was Mark's mother's way of reminding me about what had just happened. "Okay, I get it," I thought to myself and giggled a bit.

What I truly admire about the Spirit World is that it is full of surprises. In fact, the element of surprise—when people are totally thrown off and surprised by a message from someone or by someone coming through—sometimes that is really the most eye-opening, powerful, and moving experience. That man was probably the person least expecting to hear from anyone who had passed away. The information that came through for him totally surprised and shocked him.

Sometimes the people who are the most skeptical, and the most lacking believers, get the strongest, most moving messages. The reason is that the Spirit World works like an electrical system: it works in the most efficient way possible and targets the place where there is the biggest need for spiritual cleansing.

On the Other Side, our loved ones do not try to dominate or control our every move on Earth. They do not try to convince or persuade us of anything. Instead, they use their time over there to work on their own spiritual development. They transition through learning very powerful lessons that can truly be understood and comprehended only by our spiritual higher selves. However, they do continue to guide us here. They do that because on the Other Side, they have access to higher realms of knowledge and deeper insights than we can gather on this side. They continue to guide us on our soul path because they love us and care for us, and they want us to live our most authentic, true life.

# CHAPTER 10

# "LUCK BE A LADY TONIGHT"

"Gambling: The sure way of getting nothing for something."

—Wilson Mizner

Casinos are an interesting place for a psychic to be. There's always a deluge of jokes and one-liners, mostly revolving around why I can't go up to the machines and win tons of money. If I'm *so* psychic, don't I know if the roulette wheel is going to hit red or black? Why aren't there any psychic lottery winners? Unfortunately, that's not the way all of this works. First, when I get information, it's in bits and pieces. I might get a flash of something or an impression about something. But I don't get information like I'm reading it out of a book, so it would be hard for me to get specific numbers. The blessing that I have to communicate with the dead really comes from a special source, and so it's not something to use for greed or personal gains. In fact, using my abilities for financial gain adds a huge level of anxiety and shifts the energy.

About two years ago, my father's cousin invited us to a family reunion at Mohegan Sun, a casino in Connecticut. It was equidistant from some of the other places that family members were coming from. We have a pretty tight-knit, nuclear family, although I'm not very close to my father's side of the family. They live out of state, and my father was never really close to them. He doesn't have any brothers or sisters, and when his father died, the family dynamics changed a bit. As a child, my father was close to his cousins because they were mostly the same age range, and he would play with them a lot. Although we don't see them frequently, we do see them once in a while.

Because we had not seen that side of the family in quite some time, my sister Kelly and I decided to go. Of my two sisters, Kelly is more aware of my psychic gift and freely talks about it. Kara, my other sister, is a little bit more skeptical of it and more of a "believe it when I see it" type.

We arrived at the casino and immediately greeted our cousins. As we sat there talking to our cousins, a Spirit appeared at a nearby table. At first glance, I thought it was a living person sitting there, but I got a strange feeling, and when I looked closely, I could tell from the way the woman's face looked that she was deceased. Sometimes it's hard to tell if a person is living or deceased if I look quickly, but the complexion of her face was significantly drained of color. She stared longingly at me. She was older, maybe in her seventies, I guessed, with short gray hair. She wore a blue denim top with a pair of khakis. Her face looked smooth but a little wrinkled, and she had crystal blue eyes that seemed deep and powerful. She looked as though she must have passed away fairly recently because she was wearing somewhat modern-looking clothes. Of course, the Spirits can appear to me any way they want to appear, and sometimes they even alter their appearances. She waved at me and nodded. She must have known that I can connect with the Other Side. She stared at me. The sides of her face and the outline and edges of her body were very fuzzy, which also indicated to me she was a Spirit.

"You're seeing a dead person—I can tell," my sister said as we waited to be seated at the table for my cousin's dinner, her eyes following my gaze into the distance.

"What do you mean?" I played dumb. I didn't feel like explaining myself.

"You're seeing a dead person. Who is it? Who is around?" she said curiously, tugging at my arm.

"I'm not seeing anyone," I laughed. I didn't feel like getting into it. I just wanted to sit through the party, enjoy seeing my family, and didn't want to explain myself. If I explained myself, she'd ask more questions. I didn't feel like connecting today. It was my day off, and I just wanted to be alone. Though I love connecting with deceased people, they can sometimes be a little invasive if they get really excited or feel they have a really strong message that they have to get through. Mostly, however, they leave me alone.

"You can't lie to me, Tom. I've known you for twenty-two years," she laughed and rolled her eyes.

I shook my head in disagreement.

My sister took a long stare into my eyes. I knew that she knew I was keeping something from her.

"Every time you see a dead person I can tell, because you get a look over your face, and your eyes get really big. Who is it?" she said.

"Okay, fine. I just saw a Spirit around, but I don't know who it is or where she belongs, so I don't know what to do about it really. But yes, I did see a Spirit sitting across from us as we were standing here."

"I knew it," she laughed, looking in the direction where I was motioning with my eyes.

"I don't know who it belongs to," I said again. Sometimes Spirits just show up, and I don't always pay attention. Throughout my day, I can be bombarded with a bunch of Spirits.

As we sat at the table, my cousins—some of whom I really didn't even know that well—started exchanging stories with each other about upcoming births, graduations, and pregnancies. As we talked about family things, the Spirit lurked around and would roam by and wave at me. At one point, the Spirit even sat down at the table next to our family.

"Who are you?" I asked the Spirit.

"I'm for later. You're going to meet my husband later. He needs help," the Spirit communicated back to me. She smiled very lovingly toward me.

"Why are you here now?"

"I'm early—better early than late," she laughed. Her face morphed a bit and elongated, much longer and thinner than a normal human face. "I was always early in life, and I'm always early even though I am dead," she giggled again. I could see she was having some fun with me.

I could see her plain as day. She looked like an actual person, but I knew that nobody at my table could see her. She seemed so real. Besides the edges of her body form being a little bit blurry, she looked like a human form you would see anywhere—like a person who would be in a store or sitting in a restaurant. For a moment, I became oblivious that she wasn't really alive, and I started talking to her like she was an actual person.

"What's your name?" I blurted out loud. Immediately, I knew two of my cousins saw me talking to thin air.

"Who are you talking to?" one cousin asked, looking back behind her.

"Nobody," I said nervously. "I thought I saw someone."

She looked at me and furrowed her brow. "Weird," she said.

After catching up over dinner, we all dispersed to start gambling. My sister likes to play machines, and I only like to play blackjack tables. I headed toward the tables, and Kelly headed to the machines. We mentioned that we would meet in about an hour after we were done gambling. None of us are really big gamblers, and we didn't want to waste too much money.

When I pick a table to play cards, I usually sit at a table that I get a good feeling about. I can't really explain the feeling; it just comes over me. I don't know if in those moments I'm being superstitious or actually tuning in with some of my psychic powers. To be honest, I don't gamble a lot, so I don't know if my psychic powers would really help with gambling.

When I sat at my first table, there were only two other people sitting there besides the dealer. One was a young guy, kind of hip with dark hair. He had his hair slicked back, and with the number of chips in front of him, I figured he was doing pretty well for himself. There was another man there, a bit older. He had thinning gray hair. Chain smoking. He wore a tan coat with a white shirt under it and seemed relatively quiet. He wore a pair of glasses, and a Band-Aid kept the bracket together. As an intuitive, I can also feel people's energy and how they are feeling either emotionally, mentally, or physically. As I connected with this man, I felt sadness and depression.

I glanced toward his cards. The man stared at his cards shown in front of me. He had a soft 17. An ace plus a 6 card. "I'll hold," he muttered. *Mistake,* I thought. The Spirit behind him shook her head. The dealer had 12, hit with a 7, and won. Exasperated, the man grabbed his forehead and sipped down the rest of his cocktail. Even the dealer winced.

The woman Spirit I had seen before reappeared. Visually, I could see her, as if she were any of the other thousands of people trying their luck at the casino. Sometimes I just see golden lights. Thin, long, golden rays of light. Sometimes, I don't see a deceased person, but just get a sensation, feeling, or emotional communication. When I connect with those energies, I can start to feel and see information about messages that they might have or things that relate to their personalities.

I didn't want to speak out loud to her because I knew that would sufficiently freak out everyone at the table and probably get me removed from the casino, as they'd think I was speaking on a wire tap to get information about my moves at the table. But, with her just standing there, I had to figure out who she was and what she wanted so that I could somehow deal with her and enjoy my night.

Sometimes I speak to Spirits telepathically, and sometimes I speak to Spirits out loud. There's really no difference. However, in a group of people, I didn't want to start talking and appear like I was a crazy person talking to myself. As I was thinking about how to connect with the Spirit without being obvious, her voice popped into my head, interrupting my thoughts.

"Are you just going to sit there all day? Or are you going to do something about this?"

"What do you want me to do?" I asked her mentally in my head and waited for an answer. As a psychic and medium, I make it my choice to not intervene in the personal lives of others, unless I am called to do so.

"He needs to be stopped, and I need to reach him."

I suddenly got a strong feeling that she was the wife of the man who was losing. Before then, I didn't know who she was. I just knew that she was following me around, and I also knew that she was somehow connected to this man because she was hovering over him at the table. I noticed he had a wedding ring. In my mind's eye, I started to see a wedding from many years ago, and images of both the female Spirit and the guy at the table walking down the aisle of a church, celebrating their marriage.

I suddenly got a message in my head. "I guided you here to win so you would discourage him and get him to leave the table. He doesn't have this kind of money to be losing."

Another hand came around. The dealer busted, and so did the man sitting at the table, but I got an ace and a 10, giving me 21.

The man shook his head.

You wouldn't have to be psychic to see that this guy was completely losing his butt at cards, drinking heavily, and overall not very happy. He seemed very depressed and sad. Even the colors he wore were depressing and dark; he was dressed in all gray and tan, and his clothes looked worn and tattered.

Once I open up to a Spirit, sometimes the information and ideas about the Spirit start to flow in. I don't have any control over it. This is just part of the process and really how the Spirit starts to communicate and channel information through me. I was getting flashes of words, images, sensations in my body, and specific messages. *DON'T SELL THE HOUSE.* I didn't know what any of this meant, and truthfully, with the dealer standing right there, and this man losing hand after hand, I didn't think it was my place to start blurting out stuff. I also was totally not in the mood to start channeling information. I was upset that this deceased woman was stalking me. I really wanted to enjoy my night out with family and friends. I also felt I had to help this man in some way. In my head, I said a prayer to Spirit: "If it is not in this man's highest good to continue to sit at this table, please have him step away."

"I heard that!" the Spirit behind him whispered to me. Somehow she was in my head.

The next hand played out. He lost. Even though he had a few chips, he got up from the table, nodded, and headed away. The dealer silently nodded back, "All right, good luck."

I played a few more hands, won two, lost one, and also decided to end. This woman Spirit was still with me, and I felt like I needed to give the message she had to her husband.

"Go find him," she said.

"Okay, I will. Let's talk to him," I said.

The man had left the table only five minutes ago, but he wasn't in immediate sight anywhere. Logically, I figured he might be playing slot machines since he had just lost a lot of money. I walked up and down aisles of Wheel of Fortune games and saw rows and rows of cherries, fruits, and 7s. As I walked, I saw all types of people. An old woman hit a jackpot and put her cigarette in the ashtray next to her to scream a bit. "Janice, I won, I won! The wheel spun and I won!" she screamed to the woman next to her.

In crowded places, there's always a lot of Spirit activity. Funeral homes, hospitals, airports, casinos—these are energy receptacles where some Spirits love to gather. I'm not sure why casinos are such a spiritually active place for ghosts to gather. Maybe it's just that a lot of people are there. Maybe dead people like to win money, too.

Then, as I turned the corner, walking down the last aisle, I saw the man who had just been sitting at my blackjack table. I stood behind him. I watched a few spins, with no hits happening. I thought that if I didn't say something to him now, I might lose the opportunity to say something.

"Excuse me, sir?" I blurted out.

He turned around, looked at me, and turned back.

"Sir?" I said again.

"Are you talking to me? I'm sorry; I didn't realize," he said, turning back again.

"Yes, I am. And I have a very strange request. Well, not really a request, but something happened, and I need to talk to you," I said.

His eyes got big and he looked up at me more intently. "What's the matter? Is everything okay?" He started to stand up and looked around me.

"Yes, everything is fine. Don't worry at all. Sit down," I said.

He looked up at me.

"Do you know what a psychic medium is?" I asked.

"Um. Like the ones I've seen on TV?"

"Yes, like the ones on TV."

"I've seen a few of them," he said. "I don't really pay them any mind though. You don't know what they edit or do for TV."

I smiled and nodded. "Well, I'm a psychic medium, and I was getting a message for you as we were sitting at the black-jack table a few minutes ago. I didn't want to say anything to you and throw you off, and then you got up and left, so I came to find you."

He nodded. "Well, I am open to hearing it," he said. "I do believe in that kind of stuff; I've just never had any experiences." He took off his glasses and nervously began to fidget with them.

"Can you tell me what tables to play?" he laughed.

*How about none,* I thought.

I took a deep breath. The Spirit was still around me. I could still visualize her. Ready. Set. Here we go.

"I am feeling your wife around you right now," I blurted out. There's always that fear factor of being wrong.

A tear filled up in his eye. I saw it trickle down his cheek.

"How did you know I had a dead wife?"

"I'm not really sure, to be honest. She just started visiting me since I got here, and so I felt obligated to share with you. As I said, I'm a psychic, and sometimes I see and feel things about people, and I don't have a lot of control over it," I explained to him.

"Her name was Nancy. She always hated when I gambled," he laughed.

An image of a white dog came into my head, and I was being told the dog had passed away and would be a Spirit with the man's wife. I wanted to communicate this to him so he truly knew I was connecting with his wife and not just guessing that at seventy-odd years old, he had a dead wife.

"Would she be with a little white dog on the other side? Because I am seeing her with a white dog. It's small, maybe a poodle, but very small."

"Oh wow, yes. Our toy poodle, Misty. She died a week or so after my wife. I think it was just too much for her to not be with Nancy. They were very close."

That was the name I had received earlier when I was at the table, but I didn't want to bring it up right away. I wanted to ease my way into the information.

"She said you shouldn't be gambling; she's worried about the house and she said not to sell it just yet. Don't sell the house; it's all you have," I told him, repeating what I had channeled earlier.

His mouth opened a bit and his eyes lit up with surprise.

I stood with him and waited to see what his reaction was going to be.

He shook his head. A tear again came from his eyes.

"I don't know what to say. I'm just shocked."

"Is everything okay?" I asked.

We stood in silence for a minute, which is a long time to stand with someone you don't know.

"I have a major gambling addiction," he blurted out.

"I see."

"And I was thinking of putting up the house we had together for sale so I could generate some money and then continue gambling. I guess she's saying that is a bad idea, huh?"

"I guess so," I replied.

We stood silent for at least a minute. I could see him trying to process everything.

"You know, there's help for this kind of thing. You could try to overcome all this gambling."

"Yes. I'd really like to," he whispered.

"She is telling me you need to let go how mean you were to her at times. She's not upset about that anymore. She heard what you whispered into her ear at the end."

The man look stunned and said that he had a tremendous amount of guilt about how he had treated her at the end of her life when she was sick.

"I couldn't handle seeing her like that, and it really got to me," he said. "I acted in a way that I shouldn't have."

"She is saying to tell you there are no regrets."

"Tell her I love her so much," he said, visibly shaken and crying.

"She wants you to know that she loves you unconditionally."

"What's with the pictures in the wicker basket?" I asked, conveying an image that just popped into my head of a straw-looking basket with a bunch of photographs in them.

"I was just going through some pictures the other night— I keep them in a wicker basket." I could tell he was moved by this.

"That's her way of showing she is around you," I explained to him.

A lot of times the deceased people want to talk about the end, too. They want to talk about how they crossed over or things that happened at the very end. The woman Spirit started to show me a scene at a hospital, and I could see the man I was speaking to at the casino standing by her hospital bed in this image. Nancy wanted to communicate that he had made the right decision at the end by pulling her from life support.

As I could see the man in front of me absorbing the message, I could feel the woman Spirit around me fade away a bit. She seemed relieved. Lighter. The heaviness around me and the man seemed to lift a bit. I felt a chill go down my back. In my head, I heard the words "Thank you" from the woman.

I glanced back up at the man in front of me. "Thank you," he said. "From the bottom of my heart."

I turned to see if Nancy had anything more to say, but her Spirit had disappeared. I sensed she probably figured that she had passed along the message that she needed to communicate and there was nothing more to say right now. She had said what she needed to say.

When we transition to the Spirit World, we are still very much a part of the world of our loved ones. From time to time, Spirits will intervene from the Other Side because they feel they can help guide or assist with the life of someone they cared about so much on the earthly plane. It doesn't happen all the time. They will help only if they truly feel they can do something to change the outcome of the situation or impart some important wisdom. Our Spirits are always around us, and they choose to communicate when they feel we are open to receiving the messages that they have to offer us. And really, the Spirits can communicate with us anywhere and at any time—when we're at work, when we're on the subway, or even when we're at the casino. Even when we are separated in the physical form, we are still very much connected.

I never saw Edward again. And I never saw Nancy again.

About a year later, I happened to be back in that area for a conference and was sitting at a coffee shop before my presentation reading the newspaper. Strangely, I opened the newspaper and came across Edward's obituary. I recognized his picture from having met him, as his distinct look always stayed in my mind. "Edward Yin, beloved husband, father, and grandfather, passed to God's loving arms on Wednesday . . ." it began. The obituary even mentioned Edward's love of Mohegan Sun and Foxwoods. Suddenly, an image came to me of Edward and Nancy embracing, surrounded by a hue of golden light. I could feel that both Edward and Nancy were happy to be reunited with one another, and that the sadness that haunted Edward had lifted.

I guess Nancy's intervention had worked.

# CHAPTER II

# "MURDER, SHE WROTE"

"'How to Commit the Perfect Murder' was an old game in heaven. I always chose the icicle: the weapon melts away."

—Alice Sebold

Immediately, I got the sense of death as I entered the home of John Feikelson. A musty, damp feeling swam over me as I stood in the doorway to the renovated Victorian home. Though it had been mostly modernized with metal fixtures and updated, dark wooden furniture, it retained some of its yesteryear charm. But the building and the doorway felt creepy—and the reason wasn't that it was an old, spooky house. Someone had died here—John's wife, Sally. Shot in the head with a rifle, succumbing to an apparent suicide.

John was an attractive guy—fifty years old, worked out, his biceps and arms were defined and pushed against the edge of his black t-shirt. His jawline was chiseled with a light amount of facial hair, some of it brown, and some of it gray. Under his eyes, I saw dark circles. For such a strong man, I could tell he was tired, dazed, and worn out. His eyes were red, and his skin seemed more wrinkled than I remembered from seeing his photograph before my visit. He was tall, towering a bit, yet there was a part of him that seemed incredibly small— stressed and sad; he almost seemed decrepit. From his dark lines and the redness in his face, I could tell he was broken and fractured. This was a man who was sad and distraught.

John had heard about me from a friend. An admitted skeptic, John had sought me out for some advice based on the fact that his wife had died a month ago. The coroner had ruled her death a suicide. Case closed. Complete. Done. What else was there to talk about? But John was positive it was a murder. He couldn't process it first. In the midst of the funeral, police and the kids who couldn't cope but were determined to start going through her stuff and deciding what to sell and what to keep, he had forgotten everything. But now, he was ready for closure. He wanted to sell the home he and his wife had shared together, but before he could do that, he needed answers. He needed to understand the ins and outs of everything. He needed to know who killed his wife.

"I feel desperate reaching out to someone like you, but I also know that I feel deeply there is a life after death. I think if there is one, and my wife is really somewhere in the beyond, she will come through and tell us what happened. I absolutely need to know the truth," he told me when he first arrived.

For many, death is painful because of the person who leaves you. You miss the memories and the essence of the actual person. No medium can replace the connection that someone has with someone on this side. Even with the best medium, you can't hug your loved one, you can't call your loved one, and you can't go on a trip with him or her overseas. The connection through a medium is very different, even though it is a connection. And most times—as was the case with John—there is a need in my work to get closure. To get answers. To characterize and understand what someone's last few minutes were like. A medium is able to fill in the blanks when nobody else knows the answer.

For John, he didn't need just a connection. He didn't need a "Hello" or a "Did someone have a birthday in May?" He needed real, live answers. He needed to know where to search and what had happened. He needed to know if his wife had wanted to die or if his wife had wanted to live and someone else had wanted her to die.

By all accounts, John had a great life. A fearless malpractice attorney, he had made a fantastic living for himself and raised three kids in one of the biggest homes in Cambridge. Besides the accomplishments in his career, he was a noted philanthropist, donating millions of dollars to those in need and supporting numerous causes. This wasn't a family in which murders and suicides happened.

"Whatever happens, I want to know. Whatever happened, I need to be told about it. I need to know everything. I can't move on from this. And in my heart, this is the woman I love, and I know her best."

"I'm going to do the best I can," I whispered.

On the kitchen, a half-consumed bottle of water sat on the counter, next to a wristwatch. The wristwatch was face up and laid out, but wasn't ticking. A page-a-day calendar sat by the telephone and hadn't been updated in months. There was a quietness in the space. Not quite a darkness, but just a quietness. John explained that he hadn't spent much time in the property since the death of his wife.

We silently stood in the kitchen together.

"This is where she did it—well, where they say she did it," he said looking toward the wall behind me and unable to look at the space on the floor where there had been death.

John had met his wife when they were undergraduates. Sally and John were both in a course together. They flirted and became friends. Their friendship turned into a romance in their third year of college, and he asked for her hand in marriage the year after they graduated from college. They had three beautiful, successful children: a daughter, who was in medical school; a son who went on to become an attorney; and their oldest, also a son, who was in graduate school studying physics. Together, they had built a beautiful family. They had worked hard, enjoyed summer vacations, and were close-knit. Their memories were made out of trips to the Cape, campfires in the mountains, and Sunday dinners that nobody could fathom missing. John and Sally celebrated their marriage with a lot of travel and spent a lot of time together.

"I just know she wouldn't end her life. There's just no grounds. It's completely insane," John said as he began to stare at the kitchen floor in front of him. "It's senseless. She loved life. She was working on a book. We had just booked a trip to Italy. She was looking forward to so much."

I closed my eyes, began to look around the room, and took a deep breath.

"I may have to be here for a couple of days," I told John. "I want to try to get a real feel for things and really spend some quality time connecting here and see what I can pick up. This is not going to be a quick process. It's going to take a while," I warned him.

"You can stay as long as you want," he said "The important thing is just that we get answers. You can stay here, or we will get you a hotel. For now, I am going to leave you on your own so you can focus," John said, leaving the room."

I started to feel Sally's Spirit around me. A cold tingling ran down my shoulder. I had goosebumps and a chill. My head was pounding. The energy of the situation and the space were totally overwhelming me. I was having some trouble breathing. My emotions were starting to get all out of whack. I could tell this was a Spirit who was not fully at peace yet. When Spirits are at peace, they are completely at rest and relatively peaceful to interact with. In this situation, I could tell that the Spirit was still nervous, anxious, and not at rest.

Immediately, I knew answers. Somebody didn't end her life here. There wasn't sadness in this space. There wasn't depression. There was not desperation. There was fear. There was deep rage. There was anger. There was also a feeling of fakeness, lies, and deception put into me from the space.

As I stood there, Sally's Spirit started to come through me. I could feel that this was a woman who was not resolved and not happy. She had a message to communicate. Unlike many of the Spirits I run across, she was not at peace.

"It's in the writing. I wrote it all down!" the Spirit exclaimed. "Listen to me, I wrote it down!"

"Wrote what down?" I mentally communicated.

"I wrote down who killed me! Are you even listening?" she exclaimed, like a frantic person.

"You wrote it down? Where? We need to be able to find that!" I said back to her, frustrated by her lack of detail. With the tension and the energy of the situation, the lights in the room started to flicker. In the kitchen, where the dishwasher was running, it began to make a noise and shut down. Spirits actually have an energy frequency that they radiate. Have you ever been around someone and thought, *Oh, God, he is such a drain or such a negative person*? The reason is that these people give off a certain energy. Spirits are the same exact way.

"I wrote it down!" she repeated.

"Look—if you are going to communicate with me, you are going to have to slow down a bit," I said to her.

"I wrote it down!" she screamed.

"You need to relax!" I said.

"It's in the blue booooooooooooooooooooooooooooook," her voice trailed on in my head, echoing and ringing. In my head, an image formed of a blue book that resembled a small journal.

The connection between the Other Side and the Earth is a very touch-and-go one. It's not something that you can just dial up. When I connect, I have to be relaxed, stress fee, and in a mood and emotional state where I am ready to receive. If I'm anxious or not feeling well (even if the weather is bad), it can impact the connection. And it's the same for the Spirits trying to connect with me. They need to be ready and open to communicate. They need to be in a place where they feel comfortable opening up. Initially, when a person passes, for any number of reasons, that person might not be ready to provide guidance or information yet.

I could sense from this woman that she wasn't ready to communicate yet. The information she was providing was scattered and not making any sense. She seemed not ready to communicate, and I wondered if we were going to be able to really channel her in a way that provided any useful information. But I also knew that she likely felt that this was her opportunity to tell us everything and tell her side of the story. Her family desperately needed answers.

Sometimes when this happens, I ask my own guides to help me communicate with the deceased person. The reason is that my Spirit guides have a higher awareness of what's going on and work on a different vibrational level than I do. I am in my human form when I am on Earth, so my Spirit guides are closer in their connection to God and metaphysical truth. I tuned into my guides and asked them to please show me what had happened to this woman so I could help her understand and help her husband determine what was going on. I asked them to help me connect with her, and in turn, to help her connect with me. Suddenly, I had a flash of everything. I saw her buying a gun; I saw her driving home; I saw her loading the gun; I saw her slowly raising it to her head, her eyes filling with tears. "I love you, John," she whispered.

Then a loud, loud, loud bang.

I screamed, a deep yell, and slowly came back to the room. My forehead was sweating. I could feel my heart pounding heavily and strongly in my chest. My eyes were watering.

Sometimes the images that I receive in my head are so striking that they even scare me. I rarely am scared or freaked out by what I do. I think maybe one or two other times I have been freaked out by Spirit.

John appeared in the doorway, "Is everything okay?" he asked loudly.

"It's fine. Just connecting. Kind of working through things." I am sure he was sufficiently freaked out by everything, especially my screaming in a room by myself.

"Oh," he said quietly. "I'll let you be."

I sat quietly, patiently waiting for Sally to reach out to me. I began to feel a coolness enter the air. Then the room became chilly. In that moment, I was almost certain that if I blew my breath into the air, a fog would form in front of me. As I stared ahead into the empty parlor, a Spirit began to take form. When Sally had been yelling at me before, it was only an external voice with no Spirit body to it. Now, a Spirit began to form, and the Spirit was transparent—it was foggy and not immediately recognizable as a human form. First, a pale face, with short brown hair, eyes closed. Then her eyes opened. She sat there staring at me. I recognized her immediately from the photographs I had of her. She looked a bit younger than some of the recent pictures I had seen, but it's not always uncommon for Spirits to slightly change their looks once they transition to the Spirit World.

Behind her, a man stood. Stiff, frowning. He wore a long trench coat with a beret, and carried a pipe in his hand. He began to cry. In my mind, I heard loud, gulping moans that seemed haunting. He was older, and he seemed sad. In my mouth, I tasted alcohol—a strong taste of vermouth and whiskey. This Spirit was certainly older than Sally, and I could sense there was some connection between the two of them, but I didn't know exactly what it was. When I connected with the Spirit emotionally, I could feel a sense of depression and anger. I could sense that this was a Spirit who was unlike Sally: he didn't have an urgent message. He didn't have something he needed to get across or something that he needed to communicate right away. He was lethargic and feeling a bit out of sorts.

As of now, I had accomplished very little, and to be honest, I was starting to feel frustrated and hopeless. Almost six hours into my mission, nothing made sense, and nothing was lining up. Sally was telling me that things were written, but I didn't understand that message at all. I didn't know where to look, although I assumed from her statements that she had been murdered. In addition, a mystery Spirit who was with her had come through but was conflicted about really telling me anything. That had also not been helpful. I really had nothing more than a few clues that, taken together, made no sense. I sat, frustrated, in the foyer of the house—the Spirits slowly disappearing, the connection lessening and lessening. No new information was coming through.

I was here to solve a mystery basically—a murder mystery at that—and I wondered if maybe I needed to think like a detective instead of a psychic or a medium. In order to kill someone, you really do need a motive. So, I needed to ask Spirit to help me find that. If Sally was murdered, I needed to know why she was murdered.

I was confused by the information I had received. I decided to try and regroup. I wanted to seek out John. At this point, I needed all the guidance I could get. Normally, I try to keep things as separate as possible. I don't like to ask for validation or "fish" for information. I just like to say what I get, give what I see, and that's it. But I knew I was stuck this time, and that time was running out. I needed to help John as soon as possible—we needed to figure out who had killed his beloved wife.

Upstairs, I found John sitting quietly in his study. He wasn't reading or writing, but just sitting in a chair and staring out the window. I could tell that this was a man who was normally strong and confident, but this situation had captured him in a moment of weakness. It had exposed him and made him sad, scared, and desperate.

I came in and sat down with him. For a moment, we sat in silence.

"I have to ask you something," I confessed to John.

"Hit me."

"Do you know anyone who passed away who smoked a pipe?"

He furrowed his brow and thought a bit. "I am not really sure. I don't think so."

"I saw a man in a trench coat and a beret with your wife in the Spirit World. He was crying."

"Oh, that would be my father-in-law. He wore a beret and he smoked a pipe. I wonder why he is crying."

"Were you close?" I asked.

"To my father-in-law? Not at all. He wasn't really a nice person. He was a bit corrupt. But my wife was close to him, so I tried to always be nice to him."

"Corrupt?" I asked.

"I'm not really sure. He was just really strange. He was in politics. I think he did some weird things, but nobody ever really talked about it," confessed John.

The connection wasn't clear. Suddenly, I felt disconnected. Her Spirit was totally gone. She had disappeared entirely.

"Did you find anything written here? Did the police find a note?" I asked John, who sat staring out the window.

"No, there was no note. But I told you she was murdered," he said.

"I know you think that, but when I just connected with her, she told me she wrote things down. Do you have any idea where she might have written something down?"

"Well, Sally did write a lot. She loved to write poetry, journals, stuff like that. I have boxes of her writing in the attic. It's too painful to go through, though."

"Did the police look at it?" I asked.

"No, I told you; they instantly ruled it a suicide."

"We have to look for it," I said. I immediately had a sense that if we did look for it, we would find it.

"Can you ask her where it is?" John asked.

"It's not that simple. Look, it's not going to be easy, but I am telling you I have this gut instinct that if we can find this journal that she's talking about, we will get some answers. The Spirits give us information to assist us. I think it's best to listen to them."

John stared back at me, blankly, but then with a frown.

"But if we go up there, and we look for things, it's just going to make me more depressed," John said.

"Look, if there's one thing I've learned through all of this, John—through all my readings and all of my work—if there is one take-home message, it's that you should never argue with a dead person," I told him.

Silently, he nodded. "Let's go look."

We dug through boxes and boxes of stuff for three hours. We sifted through pictures, paperwork, old knick-knacks, computer equipment. Cobwebs decorated our hands as we emptied out trunks and suitcases of items.

Finally, as we were about to wrap up for the day, we came across a blue book. Immediately, I recognized it as the book I had seen in my dream of Sally the other night. It had the gold lettering on it, and it had a light turquoise coloring to it. It was exactly how I saw it during my connection with Sally earlier.

"That's it!" I screamed at the book.

John looked back at me. "What?" he exclaimed.

"That's the book—that's the book I saw in my dream!"

John grabbed the book and opened it. Over his shoulder, I could see that inside were pages filled with handwritten notes and entries. I peered over and read the entries along with him.

December 19, 1991 . . . I remain frightened for my life. Mr. L is still threatening me daily about releasing information about Dad. I fear for my life and I fear for my safety. I truly see no way out of this.

March 18, 1992 . . . My husband is starting to complain that I am spending too much time away from him. I worry about our future. Mr. L is blackmailing me now on a daily basis. He knows all about Daddy's political tricks. I'm worried about my father being taken out of office. I am doing my best to protect my father. I tried to speak to mother about it but she will hear none of it.

I could sense the trauma and anxiety in all of her writings. Frantic entries chronicling a crazy relationship with a man named Mr. L. Constantly, she referred to this man in the entries; they were almost exclusively about him. We would have to read everything to get it all sorted out and understand it. It was clear that this man Mr. L was harmful and very dangerous. Whoever he was, he could not be trusted.

"I've never seen this before. It must be her diary." John smiled, knowing we had found something that was likely about to be a major game-changer in this situation. A tear formed in his eye.

As a psychic, I saw his emotional reaction. I saw everything. I knew what was in that book would be deep and profound.

"You should sit and read it alone. I'll go downstairs."

"This will take me all night," he said.

"I'll wait," I said.

And wait I did. I went downstairs to just decompress. I needed to quiet my mind. As I walked downstairs, a sudden feeling of complete tiredness came over me. I was exhausted. I had come out on a red-eye flight. I hadn't slept in over 24 hours. I was wired but also very tired. I could feel pain in my neck and shoulders. I sat down in the living room and drifted off to sleep to the sound of Jay Leno's monologue on the TV in front of me.

I awoke to a creaking on the stairs. I could hear John coming down the stairs. There was a slowness in his steps.

"It's all in there," he said in a quiet voice as he entered the living room.

My eyebrows went up. "What is?"

"Everything you said—everything you told me; it's in the book. It's her journal."

"How far does it go back?" I said.

He plopped himself down in his chair and stared at the walls in front of him.

"Everything is in there. This is crazy."

What John told me over the next few hours really blew my mind. His wife basically had been blackmailed. Her father, the corrupt political guy I had seen earlier, had been involved in some very intensive gambling rings and white collar crimes. When he became mayor, one of his "cronies" turned on him and told him that if he didn't cough up a major amount of money, he would make sure the media outlets knew about his deceptive ways. He refused, but his daughter got involved and started a long, tormented relationship (not romantic) with this man to keep him at bay. They met once or twice a month, and she gave him financial support in exchange for his keeping quiet. Eventually, about three months before, she had cut him off completely. The journal explained how he was becoming more and more violent and irrational. When Sally's father died, she still wanted to protect his memory. But eventually it got too much. Toward the end of the journal entries, it was clear that the man had become even more uncontrollable. He was becoming reckless and danger-ous, coming to Sally's place of employment, leaving her psychotic-sounding voicemails. Then, a week and a half before Sally died, the journal entries stopped. Many times in the last dozen or so entries, she even mentioned that she deeply feared for her life.

"What are we going to do?" I asked. That was the burning question. Though we had some answers, really, this journal just brought up more questions for us. Why had Sally felt so compelled to protect her father that, ultimately, it had seemed to cost her life? How could Sally and John share so many wonderful memories together, yet she never told him anything about what was likely one of the most important, difficult issues in her life? And still, despite the fact that we had found some fairly eye-opening information, there was really no concrete proof about what had happened to Sally. Had this mysterious man carried out a vendetta on her in a fit of rage? Or had she succumbed to what was likely a tremendous amount of pressure and ended her own life? We still didn't know. The eerie image I had of her putting a gun to her head earlier in the day flashed in my head again.

Though I had found out this information and basically guided John to discover it, I was coming up blank about what had actually transpired. In my heart, I really didn't believe this woman had killed herself, but I wasn't confident. I asked someone—either her or her father or anyone who could guide me from the other side to show me something—but nobody would. There was silence.

John stared at me and suddenly began to cry. Now this was a proud man. A man's man. He was definitely not a crier. Definitely not someone who would want to cry in front of another person.

"I'm sorry," he mumbled through tears. "I just really miss her."

"I totally get it," I said. "I totally and completely get it."

I put my arm around him and squeezed him. This person needed a hug.

As we sat there, and he was crying, all of the possibilities of everything flashed in front of me. True love is one of the greatest miracles we have on Earth. It's what moves us, shakes us, and makes us exist. It brings out the core of our being, and on Earth, it's how we end up seeing each other's souls.

"We have to go to the police with this," he said.

"I agree. We should go in the morning," I said.

The next morning, we contacted the detective whom John had been in touch with. He invited us to come down to the station, and we took the journals that we had found with us. We had a detailed conversation about the contents of the journals, and the detective seemed to take our entire account very seriously.

About a month later, John contacted me by telephone to tell me that the authorities had apprehended a man. He was brought in for questioning. After a lengthy trial, he was acquitted of anything related to her murder, but charged later for blackmail, extortion, and countless other federal offenses. The case remains in the appeals circuit, but he was found guilty of many of these charges last year. I stopped following the story after I found he was put in jail.

The Spirit World guides us, comforts us, and bestows a great love upon us. At times, we need to help them by carrying out a mission or deed that they could not complete during this lifetime. Through this, we keep open the circle of communication and connection between this side and the other side. When we need answers, they are always there, and if we listen carefully, somehow they will let us know the truth. In this way, we're all mediums a little bit, aren't we?

# CHAPTER 12

# HOUSE FOR SALE

"A house is just a place to keep your stuff while you go out and get more stuff."

—George Carlin

"Do you know anything about hauntings?" my friend Michael asked me as we finished our dinner at Cafeteria—a loud, bustling place in Chelsea where the food is very Americana, and the drinks are strong. The restaurant is rather loud, dimly lit, and very happening. It's a standby in Chelsea. The ambiance is chic and clever, with lots of well-dressed men and women, and you're always liable to run into someone you know—or at least recognize from *OK! Magazine*. It's comfort food in a hip, happening Chelsea environment.

"Like places being haunted?" I asked, looking up from my food. Our waiter, who sported a sparkling glitter bow tie, came back to refill our waters.

"Yes, like homes or places where there are dead people haunting it." He cut into his medium rare steak and took a bite, shuffling some of the juices into the potatoes. "Is that stuff real?"

"I mean, I know a little bit about it, but it's not as common as you might think it would be," I said to him, taking a sip of my pinot noir.

"What do you mean by that?" he asked, I thought a bit confused by my mentioning it might be a common thing.

"Well, I mean I always go into things with a degree of skepticism. I once went to do a ghost busting for a woman in the Bronx because she thought her late husband was turning the TV on and off, and it turned out that she had an extra remote in the seat cushions that she was sitting on." I rolled my eyes as I finished the last bit of potatoes on my plate.

Michael burst out laughing. "Now that's funny!" he exclaimed.

"Kind of embarrassing when I was standing there with my holy water and my sage sticks." I smiled a bit. "Why are you asking about hauntings anyway?"

"Well, it's kind of a weird story, but do you remember Catherine? My old roommate."

I scanned my memory and remembered. Michael was one of my first friends in the city. We had met at a networking event when I first moved to the city; I didn't know anyone, so I made a lot of attempts to make some friends. When I first met him, he was in law school and lived in a rather small apartment in Harlem with two girls. Michael and I went on a date. I actually thought he was a complete jerk and never called him again, but somehow a month later, we ended up reconnecting and becoming friends. His cockiness turned into something I could handle in a friend, but maybe not a boyfriend.

I had met Michael's roommates only once or twice, but yes, I did remember Catherine. I remembered very little about her except that she was pretty conservative, mellow, and we had spent some time talking together at a party when Michael graduated law school.

"Yes, I remember her. I remember her from your law school graduation party when she was ranting on and on about Romney," I laughed.

"Well, apparently she had this aunt—who she really was very close to—and she just died this year of cancer. Catherine's trying to sell the house, but all this weird stuff keeps happening, and she doesn't know what's going on. She thinks the place is haunted," Michael confessed, chewing some of his food with his mouth open. He had the manners of a fraternity brother.

"What kinds of things have been happening?" I asked.

"All sorts of weird things. Noises, random pipes bursting. Just when you walk in there it has a really creepy energy to it—you feel like someone died there or something," he said.

"Have you been out there?" I asked.

"Yes, once right after the aunt died, and I mean, I did notice something," he confessed.

Michael wasn't exactly the most spiritual guy. Though he believed in stuff, he was also a lawyer by training and had a degree of skepticism with anything that he said or did. But for Michael to actually say that he felt something in there, that was pretty significant.

As Michael continued with the story, I heard the name Mildred in my head. It was like an external voice speaking inside my head, but I heard it very clear.

"She's been trying to sell it, but every time she gets close, the deal falls through. She really can't afford to be living there anymore," Michael said.

I heard the name Mildred again, and this time, I saw it spelled out in my head. The name continued to echo in my head. Mildred. Mildred. Mildred.

"And she's just very scared," Michael's voice had now turned to background noise with the name Mildred repeating so strongly. I wondered if someone—or something—was trying to come through.

Mildred. Mildred. Mildred. The voice was getting stronger and clearer.

"Does she know a Mildred?" I finally had to ask, or I felt this information was going to continue to disturb me. I wondered if it was connected to her or Michael. I had never given Michael a reading.

"That's the name of the aunt, I think," Michael said, stopping from cutting his steak and pausing to look up at me. He looked over his shoulder.

"Is she here right now?" Michael asked, looking around me and next to the table, mildly anxious.

The Spirit World is kind of a tough place to understand. At the risk of sounding like a George Carlin skit, I usually say that it's not there, and it's not here; it's somewhere in between. When Spirits communicate with us, they are still on the Other Side; they are choosing to be active and now communicate from there instead of existing over there—which is perfectly fine, too. So when they choose to communicate with us, in a way they are visiting us, but they are not truly walking among us because they are still on the Other Side; they are just stopping in for a visit. In truth, the veil between there and here is very thin, and they can easily travel between the two places with ease.

"I'm just connecting to the situation and getting some information," I said, not really sure how I just received that name. I wasn't really seeing a Spirit. It just popped into my head. Sometimes I even scare myself. "I'd be open to go and visit your friend. I think I could pick up more information if I was actually on the scene and could vibe things out from that perspective."

"That sounds good. I'll give her your phone number," he said.

We sat there in silence for a few seconds.

Michael sliced his steak in front of him and moved it around the plate and looked to the left and right of himself. He seemed to be preoccupied with what came through, and I wondered if he was thinking more about that than his food.

"Is Mildred still here?" he asked as he took a bite, looking up at me. "Because that was weird."

❦

The next day, Catherine called me, and we talked about the situation at her home. Catherine's Aunt Mildred was a difficult woman, and one thing that was a known fact was that she had a strong personality and could be mean, arrogant, and very particular about things. On the phone with Catherine, I could already feel Mildred's forceful energy. She was trying to organize my thoughts and get me to communicate things in a very specific way.

Catherine had served as her aunt's nurse during her long, six-year battle with cancer. Her family had abandoned her aunt after she got ill—some of the relatives wouldn't even return her phone calls. Catherine had always been close to her aunt (her mother's sister). Especially after her mother passed away.

"I know how important this house is to her," she said. "I'm worried that I am doing something wrong here. I wonder if maybe she has a message for me and she is trying to reach me."

"When I get there tomorrow, we'll figure everything out," I said.

"I'm so glad. I feel like I'm totally missing something," she said.

As I pulled into the long, winding driveway in my black SUV, a Zipcar rental, I could feel the presence of a Spirit. If I was looking for a house that was haunted, this would definitely be it. It had all the features of a spooky property, it seemed—drawn shutters, winding driveway that was escorted by several seemingly dying trees that birthed only a small number of leaves. A white-and-brown cat sat on the porch up ahead, and I could see it open its mouth to yawn and then slowly hiss. The roof was a bit dilapidated and looked to be missing several shingles. A shiver went down my spine as I pulled the keys from the ignition. I could see what Michael was talking about with the strange energy in the air.

Catherine had soft red hair to her shoulders and a small amount of freckles covering her cheeks. She wore very little makeup. Her skin was pale and soft, like the skin of a porcelain doll. She waved at me from the large farmer's porch. I remembered her face from the party, even though it had been many years ago. Her face was warm, quiet, and familiar, with round features. As I got out of the car and headed back to my trunk, she yelled from the porch, "Do you need any help with stuff?"

"I'm fine," I hollered back. I wanted to unload the car by myself because I didn't want someone else's energy touching my stuff. I unloaded the holy oil that I use to do cleansing, my sage, and candles that I make myself. I also brought with me a smudge stick and some of my angel cards.

As I walked up toward the house, I was starting to have visions and thoughts of things. I was starting to think about how strange the entire situation was and was also wondering what this aunt would want from her niece. Michael had told me that the aunt and the niece were close and she had left the niece the home in her will. From my meditation before coming out to the site, I could also sense that the aunt had been sick for a very long time. Surely, I thought they would have had time to figure out this situation before this person transitioned.

"So, tell me what's been happening briefly, and then I can try and help you," I said.

"Well, my aunt died about a year ago in this home. And I was in charge of her estate. We were very close, and I was really the only person in my family who spoke to her."

"Okay, and when she passed, you started noticing things in the house?"

"Yes, I started to notice all of this weird stuff going on in the house—weird noises, weird creeks. Sometimes we hear moans and groans in the living room. I have all these crazy dreams when I am in the house. And there have been three almost guaranteed sales that have totally fallen through. The lights flick on and off. Something weird is going on here." I could hear the anxiety and nervousness in Catherine's voice as she spoke her words so quickly and loudly. There was a tension in her body; her neck was stiff and she clasped her hands.

"So, all in all, something is up," I said, taking some notes on my pad in front of me. I didn't want to come out and say anything yet. I hadn't tuned in, and I didn't want her mind to wander. Sometimes it's better to just be relaxed at first rather than jump to conclusions. I didn't want my client to become anxious or freak out.

I could feel the fear in Catherine's descriptions to me, and I could also feel the tremendous sadness. She wanted to help her aunt. I could sense that she wanted to honor her in some way but that she was very scared and nervous, too. In some way, she felt she wasn't honoring her or that she was ignoring her. I started to feel clearly that Aunt Mildred had a message for Catherine, and she wasn't going to let her sell this home until that message was communicated.

"I think the only thing we can really do is try to connect with her and see what happens. I can't really promise anything more than that. I was feeling some stuff earlier, but I need to really just tune in and see what comes through."

"I just want this to be over," Catherine said. "This is just getting crazy. I haven't slept in weeks."

"Let's go somewhere quiet," I suggested.

She took me out to her back deck, which overlooked a beautiful lake, with some ducks swimming. One duck was quacking loudly, and the scene was incredibly peaceful and relaxing. We sat quietly for a moment. Catherine sipped on a lemonade.

I started to get connected, and she stared at me. I think she was confused as to what she was witnessing. I closed my eyes to concentrate.

Immediately, I felt the presence of a woman on the deck with us. Her presence was overpowering, and she very clearly wanted it to be known that she was there. Visually, I was not seeing her, but again, I heard the name Mildred in my head. As I said that, I also heard the name Marilyn.

"I just heard the names Mildred and Marilyn."

"Yes, well, Mildred was my aunt, and Marilyn was my mom, her favorite sister—they are both passed away," she confirmed. "And Mildred is obviously the more talkative of the two," she laughed.

I could visualize the woman connected with the name Mildred. I was seeing a strong, forceful woman—tall, heavy set, and large framed. Her hair was dark and in a bun, wrapped behind her head. She wore a black sweater with cats printed on it. I told Catherine what I was seeing. She laughed and confirmed that her aunt had quite a collection of printed cat shirts, sweaters, and outfits.

Immediately, all this information started to flow through me about the situation at hand and what was going on. I could feel so much about Catherine, Mildred, and Mildred's feeling about the home. Somehow Mildred was feeling betrayed. This emotional reaction flowed through me. I immediately felt the way I did several years ago, when I found out my own aunt had not followed the wishes of my deceased grandmother when she passed away. It was a specific emotional reaction of anger, sadness, and betrayal that I felt toward my aunt. Though Mildred's passing happened months and months ago, this memory was now totally fresh in my head. I could feel exactly how I felt several years ago. I could sense that we were moving from the validation part of the reading to the actual message that would somehow provide Catherine with some healing and comfort and allow us to figure out what was going on here. We both needed answers.

Validation is one of the most important aspects of mediumship readings. In truth, there are so many generic things a medium can say to people to give them comfort but no clear evidential information that it's really the person's Spirit coming through. When that happens, it shifts the person's perspective so clearly and so permanently that it can result in a life-changing point of view. When people come to see a medium, they don't need someone to tell them that their loved one loved them; hopefully, they knew that when the person was on Earth. Instead, they need evidence that the person's Spirit continues on.

"Well, this is weird—but this is what I am getting that there is a betrayal going on here. Your aunt is saying that she gave you this house under the impression that you were going to keep it in the family and not sell it. She's upset because you're selling it."

Catherine looked away and started tearing up. She closed her eyes trying to hold back the tears. Tears exploded down her face. She grabbed her forehead.

"I can't believe this. Is that what she just told you?" she looked up in disbelief.

"Well, I'm not making it up!" I laughed, trying to bring some humor to the situation. I couldn't tell if she was shocked because the message was so accurate or shocked because it couldn't be further from the truth.

She let her hands down, and I intuitively felt she needed a hug and comfort. I put my arm around her.

"Let's communicate with her and figure this out. If you cry, it's going to be sad, but we aren't going to get anything accomplished," I said.

"Well, here's the deal. That is true. She told me that she wanted me to keep it in the family. But financially, I just can't swing it. This place is too big, and I can't keep it in the family. Nobody wants it. It needs too much work on it and just the taxes alone are too much." Catherine seemed somewhat overwhelmed.

"I see. So you guys did talk about this a little bit?"

"Yes, we did, but I would never have had the heart to tell her that. She was suffering enough. Plus, I didn't really know until she died, and I cleared my head and realized what the finances looked like."

I think it's funny when people hide information from me as a psychic medium. Though I don't see every secret and every piece of information, I can clearly see things about people.

I wondered why Catherine had decided to keep this information from me.

"Let's see if I connect more and get any more clarification from her. Do you think that would help?"

"I think so, but I'm just so sad right now."

"Look," I said, squeezing her hand a bit. "If you want this to work out, we really need to get to the bottom of things right now. Otherwise, she will just keep haunting you, and nothing is going to get solved here. Maybe she can help you from the Other Side." I knew that we had to continue to connect with Mildred and that she would likely provide some helpful information.

"Okay," she said, taking in a deep breath. "Sounds good. I'm ready to listen. I just didn't know this would be so real."

I closed my eyes to concentrate and focused on connecting with the woman's aunt. Mildred stepped forward again. I could feel her Spirit around me, and chills started to come down my spine. I was connecting again.

"She is showing me a person. This is a living person. He's kind of short, with a bald head."

Catherine shrugged her shoulders. "I'm not really sure," she said. "I don't really know anyone bald."

"She is saying his name starts with a *Ja* sound—like *G* or *J*. It's someone in your family. One of her grandchildren."

Catherine squinted her eyes, as if she was trying to remember who the woman's grandchildren would have been.

"She wasn't very close to any of them really—but let me think. There's Ann, Pete—oh my God, Jeremy!" Catherine exclaimed. "And yes, he is shorter and bald."

"That's the person she wants you to approach about selling the house."

Catherine nodded. "Jeremy is in real estate. That's funny she would bring that up. Maybe he would be interested in doing that. I haven't spoken to him in years, but maybe he would be interested."

"Well, it all seems to fit," I nodded.

"It sure does."

"Look—I want you to follow my advice. At least reach out to him. Maybe there's something you don't know about."

"I'm going to. I really am." She was eager to take my advice.

"Do you feel a little bit better?" I asked.

"Yes, I do feel a bit better. Let's start here and see how it turns out."

Catherine's aunt started to pull back her energy. Now that Mildred had given Catherine the message, she was ready to pull away and start to transition. The sky had been overcast, but the sun began to come out.

"I'm going to sage your home, too," I said. "That way we'll make sure that you don't keep having problems in here."

Saging is a process by which I bring in a bunch of dried sage and burn it. The sage has chemical properties that clear the house. I do this for clients when they feel that there's some strange energy or hauntings in their properties.

I went into the living room and saged the entire home. It took me several hours. Toward the end of the saging process, I visualized Catherine's Aunt Mildred. She stood in the corner of the bedroom, her arms crossed.

"You think that's going to stop me? Well, it's not. I don't want this house sold."

"So, you're going to block the house from being sold and make your niece go bankrupt to try and keep it?" I said, with a bit of an incredulous tone.

"No, not at all—I don't want her to keep something she can't afford. But I also know how Catherine is. She's not thinking clearly. This house means a lot to her, and it means a lot to me. If she just sells it off, she'll regret it down the road. I want her to keep it in the family so it's still part of our legacy. My grandparents and my great grandparents lived here!"

Spirits are normally helpful, patient, and full of love—and I truly believe Aunt Mildred was doing what she was doing out of love. She knew that Catherine was making a decision that was against her word, and Catherine, being an honest person, would probably regret it down the road. She knew that by going against her word, Catherine would later suffer from guilt, sadness, and depression. Aunt Mildred wanted Catherine to honor her commitment to doing what she had promised to do.

What she said made a lot of sense.

"I get it. We're doing the best we can," I said.

"That's all I am asking for," Mildred said.

Saging doesn't work for everyone, and I guess my spiritual tear gas bomb wasn't going to work for Aunt Mildred.

When I left, we agreed that Catherine would be in touch. Though I knew she had some work ahead of her, I felt our meeting was a success. At least we knew what was going on, although it seemed a lot of questions remained unanswered.

Would Jeremy buy the place? Was he interested? Would Catherine actually call him? For a psychic, I left with more questions than I really wanted to have.

Two weeks later, Catherine left a voicemail on my machine at the office. She had called up her aunt's grandson, and indeed, he was interested in purchasing the place from her. He knew that his aunt had a close relationship with Catherine, and he didn't want to step on any toes and invite himself into buying the property as an investment. They were able to strike a deal with one another so that the home stayed in the family, but Catherine didn't have to be involved in living there anymore, as it was truly out of her budget.

"So, that's that," she said. "And now everyone is happy. I'm really happy that we can keep the place in our family, but I am not going to have to go into bankruptcy to make that happen," she said at the end of her message

Closure comes in a lot of ways for people who are passed away and their loved ones who remain on Earth—and both parties truly need closure. Sometimes when people die, for a variety of reasons, they might have unfinished business on this side. It's our job, if we can, to do whatever we can to help them carry out a conclusion to their work on this side.

The people on the Other Side do not dictate what we do or make us do things against our will. However, sometimes they do intervene if they feel that we are doing things that can be changed or altered and it's in our best interest to do so. This doesn't always happen, though, and sometimes we are forced to learn from our mistakes, and the dead have to allow us to figure things out on our own.

# CHAPTER 13

# "AND NOW YOU KNOW THE REST OF THE STORY"

"I could deny it if I liked. I could deny anything if I liked."
—Oscar Wilde

Readings provide us with information that is real and accurate. However, in order to hear a certain message, we need to be prepared and open to hearing it; otherwise, we can easily dismiss it as nonsense or completely meaningless. We need to always be open to hearing the message—we can't hear a song with earplugs in. There is a lot to be said for timing too. As a psychic, I often get only the messages that I am supposed to deliver. If someone is not ready to hear something yet or not ready to hear a certain message, it's very likely the information won't really come through. However, like most things,

"Well, anyways, she's the person that gave me your number. She's fabulous." Delores said, ignoring my statement.

I nodded.

"You know, sometimes I get messages about people, too. I'm a little psychic myself," she confessed, saying the last sentence in a tone of voice that was meant to convey eerie and creepy. She leaned in and winked at me.

"I guess we all are to some extent," I nodded.

"Well, I mean I get some really specific stuff. I like to help people. I'm *really* good," she said.

We sat silently for a moment. I could tell this woman was going to be a bit difficult to manage—in a rather harmless way, but I could just tell her personality was going to drain me. When you work with people all day, it's hard to not occasionally encounter someone who would.

"So, why are you here? I would like to know how we can work together," I said, trying to focus the conversation onto the reading at hand. I felt that her energy was distracting us from the task at hand.

I don't generally like to ask questions up front about why people come, and I definitely don't like to know particulars. I like to just go with what comes through and not guide the questions. The reason is that sometimes things come through that you really wouldn't even think to ask about. I've told people that they have health diagnoses, new relationships coming, or even big job changes with them thinking they were coming here about completely different things. I also feel that if psychics ask many questions in the beginning of the reading, it looks as if they aren't really serious.

"Why am I here? Why am I here? Why am I here?" She then paused silently, reflecting on the potential answer.

We sat silently for a minute. I didn't want to push any agenda with her or force her to say anything. I wanted to let her set the pace. We sat for a moment.

"Well, I will be honest. I lost someone very special to me several years ago. And Carmela said you are a great medium. And that's really who I would like to come through."

"I will certainly do my best," I said. "Should we get started?"

"Yes, let's do that."

"Have you done this before?"

"Yes, many times. I've probably seen over 1,000 mediums in my lifetime. The famous ones, the ones on the street, ones in other countries, ones in other places. But you know, there's a part of you that is always searching. There is a part of you that is always wanting to listen, and then a part of you that always wants to speak. It's a weird thing—having readings makes you want to have more readings."

"Okay," I said. "Well, I'm going to do the best I can."

I closed my eyes for a second to get tuned into the Spirit World. I felt two people connect with me. An older male and a younger male. I heard the name Roger in my inner ear.

"I am hearing the name Roger," I said quietly.

"That was my father-in-law," the woman confirmed. "I'm actually divorced from his son now, but we were close. I took care of him when he was dying."

As I connected further with Roger, I felt a pain in my stomach. A deep cutting like I had never experience before. It was very painful.

"I'm getting a terrible pain in my stomach when I connect with Roger," I reported.

"Yes, he died of stomach cancer. He was in quite a bit of pain."

I could hear her reach inside her purse and pull out a notebook. I heard her scribbling things down.

Then the connection shifted. Instead of getting information through visuals, I started to hear things in my head. When I say that I hear things, I like to describe that for people because it's kind of a strange thing to think about. What happens is I start to hear a voice in my head, just the way you might remember or hear things from a close friend, or the voice of your mother, or even the lyrics and sound of your favorite song. There is a tone and rhythm to it.

I heard the message "I can't believe what happened with the will. It was not your fault at all."

I shared this message with her word for word.

"Oh my God! Exactly! My crazy sister-in-law tried to change the will and then tried to convince my husband that it was me that was backstabbing everyone, but it was really her. I'm so glad my father-in-law knows that I didn't do anything wrong. She's really insane."

There was a pause for a moment. I felt Roger's Spirit pull away a bit.

"Do you get anything from the younger person?" she asked.

With the younger person, I could immediately feel there was a difference in his energy. There was more sadness. There was more unresolved. Delores almost seemed timid to ask about it. The tone she used was serious and quiet.

"I am her son," the Spirit communicated to me.

"Do you have a son that crossed over?" I asked her.

"Yes," she said gravely. "Yes, I do."

Once she confirmed she had a son in Spirit, I focused intently on trying to get a message from him. I like to first get a validating piece of information—something that really shows that it's this person. A birthday. A strange tattoo. A special memory. That validation opens up the person sitting with me to actually believing that it is this person coming through. Then the person will open up to hearing a more emotional or appreciative message.

"Oswald," I heard in a quiet tone from the Spirit World. "Oswald, Oswald, Oswald."

"I just heard the name Oswald. Is there someone named Oswald?"

"Oswald," she searched her memory. "I don't remember. It is definitely not a name my son would bring up. Keep going. See if you get something good."

A nice hit, but definitely not something to drive any point home. I needed something more.

"Tell me about a special memory," I requested from the Spirit.

Suddenly, I was in a place I had never been before. When I see scenes and images in my head, the best way I can explain it is that I see things like they are memories. It would be just like if I said to you, "Tell me about your high school prom." You might not remember every detail, start to finish, but it is likely that you would remember some key pieces of information. You might remember a flash of a color of someone's shirt; you might remember a moment when you felt uncomfortable or a special song. But you don't remember the entire thing start to finish in chronological order.

"I am going to start describing a place to you as I am being shown it. I don't know what the significance is, but I am seeing this place. It's outside. I am seeing a bench. On the bench there are some words, and there are geraniums planted all around this bench."

"I think that would be his grave site. I just planted geraniums there last week. Can you read the words on the bench?"

"I'm trying," I focused intently. I kept losing the image in my head. I was having trouble holding it.

"That's all . . . That's all folks?"

"Oh my God. Yes, that's it. That's what he wanted on his grave stone. He joked about it all his life. Of course, we never really thought we would ever have to deal with that," she confessed, as I heard her reach for a tissue.

Though I knew she had connected with her son before, I felt within me that this reading would be different for this woman. I knew we were going to go deeper. There was more of this man's story to tell. I could feel that he was holding back. I also wasn't entirely confident in how competent the mediums she had consulted with before had been. I was tempted to think that her being a "psychic junkie" of sorts really meant that many of her readings were less than quality. She had asked many questions before and had many readings before, but today, I felt she might actually get some answers.

I'm not trying to say that the other readings she had before didn't mean anything, as surely they had. But I knew that this reading was going to go deeper and be more intense.

"I need to talk to my Mom," the Spirit said to me. "I need her to know how I really died."

The Spirit seemed to be shy and retreat after he communicated this. Maybe—I thought—he wasn't ready to communicate yet. He was still holding back a little bit.

"I think he wants to talk about his death. The way he died," I said.

"Okay. I am open to hear anything. I know how he died though. But he can talk about whatever he wants."

The Spirit that I was visualizing in my head said that she didn't know the truth. And now was the time for truth. I suddenly got the impression of an overdose. I was feeling dense, dark, drug energy and felt pressure and congestion on my throat and nose.

"Your son . . . he . . . had an overdose. He died from an overdose of drugs."

"No, he died from a food allergy," she said abruptly. "Lobster," she added.

"Well, he's telling me an overdose. He said he is ready to talk to you about this now."

"My son never did drugs in his life," she said matter-of-factly.

I paused for a moment.

"Let me tune back in and see what else I get," I said.

Together, we waited patiently. I was eager to make a connection deepen, so I could communicate what this Spirit obviously wanted to tell his mother.

"Tell me what you want to tell her. Just tell me," I communicated to him.

"She's right. I never did do drugs. But I experimented with things, and it backfired. It's all my fault, but I need to tell her what happened. I need to give her closure," the Spirit said.

"What he is telling me is . . . ," I said, not finishing my statement, and interrupted by her.

"No, you listen to me, Mr. Famous Psychic. My son never did drugs in his whole life. He got a 3.9 GPA from Yale University. He worked in finance, and he had a baby on the way. He never did drugs—you hear me?" she said to me in a shrill voice.

My eyes popped open. "You need to relax," I said calmly.

"Don't tell me to relax. My son is dead, and you are blurting out he is a drug addict? You should be ashamed of yourself. I want my money back." Her tone was hostile, angry, and completely irate. She was actually spitting a bit as she talked.

"I can assure you—I am just giving you what I am picking up." I started doubting myself. I started questioning myself. Usually, I see things so clearly, and I never doubt what the Spirit World has to tell me or wants to share with me. I was going to try to focus a bit more.

"If I'm going to believe this, I'm going to need some more validation. I mean, for ten years, I've believed he died of a food allergy. Why is this being changed now? This isn't right. I think you are having an off day."

A light rain started to pour outside, and I opened my eyes to reset my connection. The mood was shifting in the room. I questioned the Spirit. Was this woman really ready to hear what I had to tell her? Was she in a place where she could truly process what was starting to come through? For some, living in denial and fear is a safer place. Maybe that was where she needed to be.

The thing with readings is that people often believe what they want to believe. Part of me wondered if the Spirit had really come through with this information or if Delores had taken bits or pieces of information and translated it into what she wanted to believe or hear. I wondered if maybe this information had tried to come through before, and she had just ignored it and pretended it wasn't there.

"Well, let's not get upset," I said. "Let's just see what comes through." I wanted her to be calmed and relaxed, because I know from doing readings that if people get nervous or anxious, it can upset the entire flow of a reading.

"Talk about what? This reading is horrible," the woman said, looking away as she insulted my work and frowning. She grabbed her pad, pulled off the sheets, and ripped them in half. My heart was racing, and I was insulted she would do such a thing.

I knew the accuracy of the information I was getting. I knew that I wasn't just hearing things that weren't there. I was being told specific, accurate messages from the Spirit World, and I knew the information I was getting was totally correct.

"Look, I think we need to take a step back for a second and just relax. You're yelling at me, and that doesn't make me comfortable at all," I said sternly.

We both sat there. The rain that was dotting the windows was slowly trickling down and seemed peaceful. My stomach began to twist and turn.

"Now if you want to hear what I have to say, I want to tell it to you. But if you are going to yell and insult me, we're going to just have to stop, and I will give you back your money."

She looked at me and sneered, "I'd like that very much."

I was surprised she took me up on my offer. I've said this before to clients when they have truly frustrated me and I really felt they needed to be grounded back to reality. It usually shocks them because they realize how inappropriate they are acting, and they relax. I guess in this situation, she was too upset.

I reached into my wallet and pulled out some cash that I had—it was enough to give her for her reading. I put it on the table in front of her.

"You're terrible. Carmela was totally wrong," she said as she grabbed the money from the table.

"I think you should go now," I said. I was starting to feel uncomfortable and almost unsafe.

She stormed out of the office, slamming the door behind her.

"Remember Oswald," I muttered to myself. She was long gone.

Over the next few weeks, I felt betrayed by Spirit. I wondered why Delores's son had come through with information that his mother was so clearly not ready to accept. She obviously didn't want to hear that, it obviously didn't help her, and she ended up storming out without talking to me. I couldn't get past it. The entire thing stuck with me like a bad date that just ended horribly. It lingered. I continued with my readings, but I wasn't as enthusiastic. I felt betrayed by a best friend.

Something I trusted in so much. I almost felt like everything I had come to believe and understand was totally fake and wrong.

About a week after Delores Martin had stormed out of my office, the phone rang.

"Hello, this is Thomas John," I answered the phone. It was a Monday morning, and I was in the office early to catch up on paperwork.

"Thomas?" the voice said back quietly.

"Yes, this is Thomas. Can I help you?" I thought I recognized the voice.

"Thomas, this is Delores. I had a reading with you the other day."

"Yes, I remember. What can I do for you."

"Well, Thomas, I wanted to apologize. First and foremost, I am sorry for how I acted last week. It wasn't right of me to speak to you that way."

"I understand." And in a way, I did understand. Frankly, it was a situation that made complete sense to me. She was not ready to hear and receive what I had to share with her. She felt scared and probably, since she had seen many psychics and mediums before who had never told her this, there was a sense of disbelief.

"I also wanted to validate that some of the things you said were right. Actually, the last week was a whirlwind, but some really bizarre stuff came out. I wanted to come back and talk to you. Would you be open to that?"

I thought about it. I could sense this was a woman who was authentic and meaningful in her apology. I couldn't deny her the opportunity to hopefully reconnect with me, and her son, and make sense together out of what had happened.

"Of course," I said. "Can you come in next Monday at 10 a.m.?" I glanced at my schedule.

"I will make it work," she said.

I opened the door to my waiting room. Delores sat nervously reading a newspaper and biting her nails. As the door opened, she put the paper down.

She was dressed in the same style as before—large hoop bracelets and heavy gold jewelry on her hands and fingers. Gold rings covered her left and right index and middle fingers—two or three on each finger. She wore a long black sweater that wrapped around her shoulders and back, and a dark pantsuit. This time, her blouse was more low cut, revealing a tattoo of a dove with a date on it.

One thing I have learned in this work is that empathy hurts, but compassion always heals. Empathy is all-consuming, draining and, in a way, can slowly erode us and kill us over time. It robs us blind of our own emotional experiences and makes us forced to take on someone else's. Compassion is a way of being engaged but distanced. It's a way that, as a healer, helper, teacher, or person of the world, we can most help others in need.

I could feel that Delores was in a different state of mind. She was ready to listen and to receive the information that I was getting. She wasn't in a mood to be judgmental to me. She wanted to heal and move forward.

"I want to apologize to you. I was completely wrong the way I acted. You were trying to help me, and Spirit was trying to help me, and I completely shut it down."

"No, it's my fault! I should have gone slower—I should have known you would need to digest everything. It's just that when I get information, it comes through to me so fast." I truthfully did feel that I should have somehow realized that she wasn't ready to hear what I had to say yet.

"What you told me was true. Do you remember telling me the name Oswald?"

I searched my memory. "Yes, I do remember that—vaguely, but I do remember that." I usually don't remember details, but in this situation I did because the name was sort of unusual.

"Well, I never heard that name really, but when I got home, I remembered he had a friend Oswald. So I made a few phone calls, and it turns out that Oswald was the person that my son last spent time with before he passed. Well, after a lot of research, I tracked him down, and we had lunch—and he basically validated what you said. My son didn't use drugs, so I was so shocked by you telling me this, but he was . . ." her voice trailed off as she began to cry.

"He experimented that day and I guess it didn't end well for him," she added, trying to hold back tears.

"I'm so sorry to hear that," I exclaimed. I was surprised to be hearing this. Here was a woman I figured I would never see again, and not only was she here, but she also was talking to me about how my reading of her situation had been accurate.

"It's okay. I was sad about it, but I've actually totally made peace with it. I'm just glad that I know the truth instead of thinking that he died from something else. I needed closure, and you know, I think in the back of my mind, I always knew something didn't fit."

"But you needed to hear it from your son probably. You needed that validation."

"Yes, I did. I didn't want to believe it. And you know, I do miss him, and I do feel upset he decided to experiment with drugs, but I truly feel it was an accident and not intentional."

"I agree—it wasn't intentional," I confirmed.

Some secrets we outrun, but others run right toward us. Sometimes messages are healing, and sometimes they are truth baring. Sometimes we really need to hear details. The nitty-gritty. The dirt. The grime. Denial works for a while, but not forever. After a while, we become unhinged by it. By knowing the truth about someone's passing, we can begin to heal, grieve, and mourn that person's loss.

Delores left my office that day knowing the truth about the passing of her son. And while it might not be what she had wanted to hear at the beginning, people say that the truth will set you free. I wondered if, in her heart, Delores had always known that something didn't make sense. Regardless, now she was ready to continue on.

# CHAPTER 14

# DYING TO BELIEVE

"A family is a place where minds come in contact with one another. If these minds love one another, the home will be as beautiful as a flower garden. But if these minds get out of harmony with one other it is like a storm that plays havoc with the garden."

—The Buddha

The phone rang at 7:04 a.m. I forgot to turn off my office call forwarding on Friday night. It was Saturday morning. I was hung over. The phone rang a second time. The caller ID displayed a 212 area code. "DEVERAUX, D." Lounging on my sofa, wearing nothing but glasses and black boxer shorts, I answered on the third ring. I wasn't quite sure why I'd answered—but I answered.

"Thomas . . . John," I said, clearing my throat in between my first and last name.

"Oh, hi!" a woman's voice enthusiastically greeted me, almost surprised to be speaking to me and not my machine. "Is this Thomas John?" I could tell she sounded slightly concerned that she was calling so early on a Saturday morning.

"Yes, this is he. What can I do for you?" I answered warmly, trying to put her at ease.

"Hi. My name is Daisy; I found you online. On Best Psychic Directory."

"What can I do for you?" I asked, somewhat rhetorically, already feeling a deceased younger energy coming forward; an image of a rope flashed in front of my eyes. It was too early for this. Why did I answer the phone?

"My son passed away yesterday; well, three days ago, it seems like yesterday. I need a reading. I need to make sure he's okay, and I need closure." I noted that she seemed almost upbeat as she told this story. She conveyed the story in a proud and positive tone.

"Let me look at my schedule. I usually book up quickly, but let me see what I have." I reached to my coffee table to get my appointment book. "You know, oddly enough, I have a cancellation at 10 a.m. on Tuesday morning. Would you want that appointment? Otherwise, it could be a bit of a wait," I told her.

"Could you do 10:45?" she asked.

"No, I have someone at 11:15. If you want the full experience, we should do an hour."

"I'll move something around. I have a manicure, but I'll change it."

I silently noted the strangeness of her response. File your nails or talk to your dead son? Was there a choice?

On Tuesday morning, I couldn't find my keys or the tax documents I needed for my after-work appointment with my accountant. I had attended a charity event the previous night and had not taken the time out to organize myself for the meeting. This morning, I couldn't find anything. After a frustrating hour of searching, finally, things started to turn up. Even the cab I called to take me to my first appointment was a hassle due to backed-up traffic on the nine short blocks we had to travel north on 7th Avenue heading up to my office from my apartment on 20th Street. I wondered if I was being blocked. Was I not supposed to read this woman? Everything seemed unnecessarily onerous and deceptively difficult. I somehow managed to arrive only five minutes late and raced into the elevator. She was waiting when the doors opened on to my floor.

"Sorry I'm late," I said. She wore oversized sunglasses and had blonde hair up in a tight bun. Her off-the-shoulder floral silk shirt matched her skirt. She was tall, thin, and tanned. Her teeth were pristine and white. She smiled as the elevators opened, the way you might greet your maid when you are about to dump five loads of laundry and a filthy kitchen on her. She had on very little make-up, only lip gloss. My first reaction, honestly, was that she looked way too put together to have a dead son. She looked like a movie star.

"It's okay," she said, laughing. "I'm just nervous."

I headed into my office. I put down my coffee, iPod, and briefcase. I said a quick meditation and walked to my office door to properly greet my client. As I went toward the door, I stopped. A Spirit had arrived—a young man—I could see him clearly: brown hair, bushy eyebrows, a round face, casually dressed in a flannel shirt and jeans. I spun around quickly, not certain if this was someone in my office or a Spirit.

"I'm dead," he said.

"You're right—you are. Are you okay?" I asked.

"As okay as I can be for a dead guy," he smirked.

I didn't reply.

"Yes. But she's not," he added.

"I'm preparing to start. Wait here." I said, somewhat annoyed. "Why are you here ahead of the appointment anyway?" I had rules with Spirits, and arriving before the reading had begun was a major no-no.

"I'm not. You're late. This is my first time."

I turned away from him. I knew if I continued to connect with him, he would sap all the energy I needed for the reading. I lit a candle on the table, said a quick protection prayer, and finally went to get my client.

"Come on in," I said, opening the door to my private office.

The woman came in and sat down. "I need to know that he's okay. That's all I need to know."

"I understand. Let me tell you how I work. I am going to try to connect with your son. I can't promise he will come through, and other Spirits might come through. I need to ask you to be respectful of the process. Now, if your son does come through . . . " An unexpected and loud grating sound emanating from the heater cut me off, startling me. "Now, if your son does come through—he might identify himself with memories, dates, names, all sorts of things. Everything might not make sense, so I would advise you to write down whatever you want to remember."

She nodded her head in silent understanding.

The room felt cool and crisp. It is common for a Spirit's presence to significantly lower the temperature of a localized area, and now was no exception. The hair on my arm stood at attention. I immediately felt a male presence. I can distinguish male from female energy because their textures are so different. Masculine energy is darker and heavier, wider and deeper. It takes up more of a physical presence; it almost feels like a heavy steam that makes it difficult to breathe, like in the sauna. The Spirit remained. His unearthly form pressed right up against my face. A shiver ran down my spine. The heater squeaked.

"Is that him?" she asked.

"I don't know," I said.

"The first thing your son wants you to know is that he's fine. He's found his grandmother; he found her. P? Paula?"

"Paulette! My mother! Oh thank God!" She exhaled deeply in relief. "Is he okay, Tom? Is he going to be okay? Is he going to make it to Heaven?" Her voice was full of urgency.

"Who is Jason?" I continued. I was not intentionally unresponsive to her questions, but once I am receiving information from Spirit, I usually can't just turn it off.

"Not Jason—Justin."

"Don't give me any information," I said quickly. "I'm the medium; let me tell you things."

"I am seeing Jason," I started again. "He's with Jason."

"Jason . . . Jason . . ." I could see her scanning her memories. She closed her eyes. Her eyes twitched a bit. She touched her forehead. "Jason! Oh my God, that's our little cousin! I didn't even think about it! He died from cancer three years ago. We weren't very close relatives—it's my brother's wife's sister's kid—but Justin and he were actually quite close. He called him Daddy."

Seemed like it could make sense. I moved on quickly. "Why am I seeing Kit Kat bars?" I asked.

"Oh my God—Justin's favorite! Always candy bars. Tell him I put one in the casket. Oh baby, I love you, Justin," she cooed. "Can he hear me?"

I try not to lie. I have instincts and hunches, but truly, I don't know the answer.

"What I am seeing is . . . ," as I tried to make sense of the image I was seeing—something red and brown—she was busy scribbling notes to herself. *What is she writing?* I wondered what comprised the paragraphs she was recording when I had barely spoken but a few names and phrases. "What I am seeing is . . . ," I continued.

"Spit it out already," she said. She immediately seemed to regret her outburst. "Sorry."

"It's fine. I understand." And truthfully, I wasn't mad. Her son had just hung himself. I couldn't begrudge a little attitude.

"He keeps showing me this long rope. He said he used a rope—a jump rope, and he's sorry he broke the lamp?"

"Yes, he hung from the . . . ," she stopped herself.

Then she emitted the loudest cry I had ever heard. It was a wail of sorts—like the sound of a mother whale searching the deep ocean for her lost calf. If you lose a parent, you're an orphan; a husband or wife, you're a widow or widower; but there's no title someone earns for losing a child. It's simply too painful to describe in a mere title.

"It's my fault. I caused this," she said.

I turned to the Spirit next to me to retrieve a message. "In a way she did; I asked for help for years. But she couldn't see my suffering. It's not her fault. Tell her not to blame herself," the Spirit said.

"He's saying that part of this was evident; he did give you signs that he was in need of help. But he doesn't blame you," I translated.

"There was one time, when he was sixteen when he tried to . . . ," her voice trailed off into a story as an image of a stick of glue, of all things, flashed through my consciousness.

"Sniff glue," I blurted out, completing her sentence.

"Yes, that's what he did," she rather sheepishly admitted.

"Tell her that she needs to stay on Earth. She can't be with me," the Spirit urged.

"Your son is saying you belong on Earth. You're not passing away. Don't do anything stupid," I warned.

"Is he worried that I will?" she asked, a puzzled look on her face.

*"Everyone has control over their own destiny,"* the Spirit asserted.

"He's saying that in a way we all manifest our own destiny," I offered.

"I won't," she said quietly.

"Did you bring a picture of him with you? He said you brought one and you were hoping I would bring it up."

"Yes, I did," she said. She burst into tears and put her hands around her face. "I'm sorry this is really intense."

I pushed a box of tissues toward her. "It's perfectly normal to cry. Let it all out. Don't worry—the dead people aren't going anywhere. Take the time you need." I didn't want to rush her, but information kept coming and I didn't want to lose any of it so I continued. "Is it a picture of him in a swing set?" An image of a child swinging flashed into my mind's eye. I even heard a child's laughter.

"Yes—oh my God, Tom! Is he okay? I need to know," she whispered to me.

"He's making his transition—he will be fine, he's where he needs to be. He went quickly. Don't worry about the pain."

"I was worried about that," she admitted.

"He wants you to forget about any bad times you endured as a family; the drama, the divorce. He forgives you for everything."

She nodded her head.

The session wrapped up with a few more validations. It was comforting toward the end, and it seemed to slow down. Justin pulled back his energy; he stopped coming on quite so strong.

"I'm starting to lose the connection," I warned her, as the room started to warm.

Sometimes toward the end of a reading, to ground myself, I need to eat some carbs or some sugar. I reached into my backpack and grabbed the granola bar from the front flap. I took a bite. I felt some warmth return to my face. A shiver ran down my spine. During a reading, I become so connected with the Other Side that it starts to drain my life force. Sometimes it even feels as though I'm leaving the Earth plane for good. The sugar, aside from preventing me from passing out, also seems to reconnect my Spirit and my physical body. Just as I finished eating, he said one more thing.

"Tell my mother that she needs to worry about herself more than me."

I shared the message. She nodded. He was in a better place now. He could shut the door; we had to sit here and pick up the pieces. We stared at each other. My brow was sweating. She wiped her face. We sat together for a few moments. It was quite strange. We basked in that awkward atmosphere, the afterglow that followed most "successful" readings. We sat there, absorbing the intimacy of this emotional process and each of our contributions to the experience. A reading is like a drama, with a distinct beginning, middle, and end. The climax, that was the death that brought us together.

"Thank you for doing this—especially on such short notice," she said.

"It's my pleasure. It's my job." I smiled kindly at her.

"Thanks. It really helped me to believe." She paused. "Can I ask you something?"

I nodded.

"When I go, will he be there?"

"Yes, you will be together. Our loved ones greet us on the Other Side."

"I guess I will have to wait. It sounds nice, though." She looked at me, almost longingly. "Can I give you a hug?"

"Of course," I said.

On Friday mornings, I usually go into the office late, at around 11:00 a.m. I was surprised to get a call from my assistant at 9:45 a.m. I was on the treadmill, just starting my third mile (I try to work out every morning).

"The police are looking for you," she whispered quietly. "They're here and they are looking for you."

"For me?" I asked. Random thoughts raced through my mind.

"Yes, they are saying it's about a client. They won't tell me anything else."

"I'll be there as soon as I can, but I'm still at the gym," I said, "It could take me an hour." Then I caught myself. *Am I crazy? The police are at my office!*

"I really think . . . ," Kelly's voice trailed off.

"I know, I know. I'm sorry—I'm coming right now." I stopped the treadmill, jumped off, and raced right out the door in my sweats.

I hailed a cab on 14th Street and headed directly uptown to Chelsea. Thoughts flooded through my mind as I charged into the lobby of my office building. I tried to tap in to a vision of the scene I would encounter upstairs. But this is the thing about being psychic: you rarely can channel messages for yourself, and barely ever on command. You are simply too close to the situation; your own emotions act as a barrier, insulating you from the psychic information stream when it comes to your own life. As ironic as that may be, it's just the way it is.

As the elevator doors opened on the sixteenth floor, two plain-clothes detectives sitting in the waiting room came into my view. If there were an award for "odd couple of the year" at the police station, this pair of detectives would be the annual winners. They were polar opposites: the young one was six foot three, muscular, with tattoos and a defined jawline. The other was short, round, pale, and unkempt. I mentally prepared for what I was sure would be yet another in a long list of odd encounters I've experienced in my line of work over the years.

"Hi, I'm Thomas," I said, catching my breath. As I approached the odd pair, extending my arm to shake hands, they arose from their seats.

"Hi, I'm Detective Caprini," the shorter one said as we shook hands, "and this is Detective Mulligan," pointing at the rather intimidating, sunglass-wearing man to his left. "Look, I'm sure you don't know what's goin' on here. You're not under suspicion, and there's no reason for you to be nervous. We're gonna make this as easy as possible on everyone involved— including us." He motioned toward my office, "Do you mind if we have a word in private?"

"Of course not—by all means." I led the way into my private office. "Please have a seat," I said, motioning toward the "client couch," wondering which of them had prompted this visit from the NYPD. As I sat down, I asked, "Can I get you gentlemen a cup of coffee? Tea? Or perhaps a water?" Both men, one looking more tired than the other, replied "Yes" without skipping a beat. I buzzed Kelly on the intercom. "Could you bring the detectives each a coffee?"

Detective Caprini cleared his throat. "I am gonna cut to the chase here. Daisy Deveraux is dead." He peered into my eyes after a long, uncomfortable pause, examining my face for a reaction to his revelation. Just then Kelly opened my office door, tray in hand, and set cream and sugar in the center of the coffee table and a cup of coffee before each detective.

"Will there be anything else?" she asked. I shook my head and she turned and left, closing the door quietly behind her.

Detective Mulligan, whipping a small Moleskin notebook and uncharacteristically tasteful Mont Blanc pen from the inside pocket of his black suit jacket, picked up where Caprini left off. "Thing is, you're one of the last telephone numbers in her cell phone. She had an appointment with you this past Tuesday, the 14th, correct?"

"Yes. Yes, we met on Tuesday. I had only just become acquainted with Ms. Deveraux when she called me on Saturday morning, but I was able to accommodate her rather quickly because I had a last-minute cancellation." I tried to explain the situation as thoroughly as possible, still wondering to myself, *What the hell happened?*

A quizzical look on my face must have betrayed my thoughts as Detective Caprini immediately answered the question I asked only in my mind. "She hung herself. Nasty scene; we've been at her penthouse since 3:00 this morning. It's a clear-cut suicide, but her sister is calling for a full investigation . . ."

" . . . and so we need information about Ms. Devereaux's movements this past week," Detective Mulligan interjected, rather rudely. "Did she come to you to talk about the death of her son?"

"She's dead?" I asked stunned. I leaned back in my chair.

"Yes," the short one said, looking over at his partner and winking.

"I talked to her about her son. He had passed away a couple of days prior to her reading, and she needed to receive a message from him. We talked for about an hour. She seemed to get a lot out of it."

"You talked to her son?" the short cop asked.

"Yes, I channeled him and talked to him. I'm a medium. That's what I do; I speak to the dead."

Detective Caprini smacked his lips and rolled his tongue on his front teeth. The other one stared at me and then slightly adjusted his flag pin on his pocket.

"So what is it that you do?" the taller cop asked.

"I talk to Spirit people. I talk to the Spirits of those that aren't here anymore."

The shorter cop scribbled onto his pad and scrunched his nose.

"Some people can do that," the taller cop said.

The shorter cop stopped writing and looked up at him, staring.

"There *are,*" the taller cop emphasized.

"Did she seem distraught?" the short one asked. "Upset? Angered?"

"No, she was relieved. We connected with her son, I told her a lot of things, she was happy. She even acted better—I mean, I don't even know what I am saying—she just seemed better. She looked better. She was definitely not upset leaving here," I said, almost pleading.

"So, you didn't see this coming?" the taller cop chimed in.

I was silent. The taller cop, who had seemed to be mildly defending me during the interrogation, had just turned on me. He had connected the dots. Person comes for reading. Person gets reading. Psychic says person looks and feels great. Person commits suicide days later. Guilty. Not to mention isn't a very good psychic.

"Well?" the other cop said. He seemed to smirk a bit and didn't blink.

I refused to engage in this and ignored the question.

"We'll be in touch," the short cop added, and handed me his business card as he pushed past me to the door of my office. "Come on, Mulligan, let's hit it."

The tall cop followed his lead without making eye contact.

As the elevator doors shut on the officers, thoughts raced through my mind. I had been betrayed. Was this a sick joke, some kind of stunt? Visit the psychic, trick him into revealing the afterlife to you, and then promptly go there? I was enraged and upset. Hurt and humiliated. Daisy had claimed to be so comforted by the messages she received. I did everything right, according to the code of ethics I had developed after years of consultation with clients.

When she had come into my office, Daisy was silent, awkward, and stiff. She was hardly even breathing, for heaven's sake; it was as if her lungs had collapsed. Conversely, after her reading, there was a spring in her step; her natural elegance had returned to her body. When she left my office, Daisy seemed at peace and finally able to mourn her son gracefully. What I had done had worked. She had left so much in my office—so much toxic, negative energy—it had felt so dark and heavy when she left that I had to cleanse the room with sage not once but twice. Still, I was happy to be a conduit for removing this energy from her aura and lessen her burden. How could she betray me like this? Had I missed something? Had I been so involved in delivering messages about swing set photographs that I had missed her cries for help—the way she ignored her son's subtle hints for years?

For a moment I entertained a horrible notion: had I pushed her over the edge? Had my reading—which I felt had been on target—been so convincing that Daisy had decided to join her departed son because she was more confident in the existence of the Other Side? Had I tempted her? Maybe she figured, *If Justin made it to the other side and was even able to talk to me after ending his life, can't I do the same?*

A rumbling in my stomach and an intense pain washed over me. I felt my face get pale and clammy, and a thick sweat started on my forehead. I looked for the nearest bathroom. Though I practically live in my office, I almost forgot where I was. I ran toward the bathroom door, and just as I opened it, I began to vomit.

I canceled all my appointments for the day. The thought of giving a reading to anyone filled me with dread. Thankfully, I was off all weekend as well. I needed a break, some time alone to think. I needed to make a plan. I didn't leave my apartment for the entire weekend. I was scared, but I was also angry. I ordered take-out and watched reruns of *Friends*. I didn't answer the phone, check my email, or interact with anyone. Client phone calls and emails were piling up. I didn't want to give another reading ever again. This time, I was really done.

I wanted to go the funeral but didn't. I didn't know how to deal with the entire tragic situation. I wanted to bury it so deep inside that I would never have to think or hear about it ever again. What lesson was this supposed to be teaching me? I had so many questions. Should I have seen her immediately the same day that she called? Should I have told her she could call me whenever she needed?

A week after the funeral, the police called to tell me they didn't need me for any further questioning and that they wouldn't be contacting me anymore. The cop told me they discovered my client had been planning her suicide long before her son took his life. They found several drafts of a suicide letter on her computer dated two weeks *prior* to her son's suicide.

"I shouldn't be telling you any of this, but I wanted to give you closure and assure you: you did *not* cause this tragedy," Detective Mulligan admitted. The relief was overwhelming, but it didn't resolve the deep sense of guilt that still plagued me deep inside.

Five weeks later, I still felt haunted by Daisy's Spirit. I would see her in my dreams, but she said nothing. I tried contacting her Spirit, but she didn't come through. I canceled reading after reading; I was distracted, and my readings are not on target when I am in such a state. My need to understand what went wrong overpowered my characteristic compulsion to work. What had I missed? If she had been planning a suicide all along, surely, her son should have warned me. Why didn't I get any impression, any message at all? Did no one want to try to save her by warning me? Come on Spirits, own up! Not knowing what to do, and almost without thinking, I looked in my phone records, found Daisy's number, and called it. I don't know what I was expecting. Maybe I just wanted to hear her voice on an answering machine.

On the third ring, someone answered.

"Hello?" a woman said.

A knot formed in the pit of my stomach. "Hi, who is this?" I asked.

"Um . . . well you called me. Who is *this?*" the woman asked.

"This is Thomas. Thomas John. I am trying to find out about Daisy."

"Daisy's dead, she died about four weeks ago. There's really nothing more to say. Have a g—"

"I killed her," I interrupted. The words surprised me.

"I'm sorry?" she said.

"I killed Daisy. Well—I might as well have killed her. I can't go around carrying this guilt. She came to me for a psychic reading two days before her suicide."

"You're the psychic that read her?" the woman said, with a tone that made it clear she had heard the account of our meeting.

"Yes," I whispered.

There was silence for thirty seconds or so.

"When we talked, she seemed fine. But I should have seen this coming," I said.

"You know, I don't see it that way," the woman said.

"It feels as though I was the last person who could have helped her," I said.

"She had many years of chances. I'm her sister, Eileen. And I understand what you do. I get it. I believe in it. And trust me, I didn't always get my sister, and I didn't always agree with how she lived her life, but I knew her very, very well. What you did truly helped her. Daisy was dead before she ever called you. She was so furious that Justin stole her thunder by committing suicide before she had a chance to. I know it's a terrible thing to say, but I know in my heart it's true. She was planning it—for weeks, maybe months. She didn't come to you at a fork in the road. She came to you at the end of her journey."

"But I still feel totally responsible."

"You shouldn't. Daisy made a lot of choices. You know, sometimes things are larger than life. There's only one, single, solitary person in life who can control our destiny, and that is us. Besides that, it's all bologna," she laughed.

Eileen and I talked for about an hour. She told me Justin's life was a rollercoaster, and that was, for the most part, due to the influence of his mother. Daisy drank, and when she got angry, she'd beat him. His father, an alcoholic, left a month after he was born. She read me a few passages from Daisy's diary and shared tidbits of their life together. We finished up, and I thanked her for taking the time out to speak to me and for helping to restore my peace of mind.

That afternoon Daisy visited me. She stood in my bedroom as I folded my laundry. I stared up at her, startled and confused. She looked peaceful and serene. She was dressed not in loud paisley or bright colors, but in an elegant white gown.

"Why are you here?" I said coldly, my heart beating loudly.

"I came to tell you why I did it." I watched her run her finger along her long blonde hair, now hanging past her shoulders, instead of up in a tight bun like the day she had visited me in my office. The voice of her Spirit was as clear as the annoying DJ blaring from the radio on my nightstand. I reached over and shut it off.

We were silent for a long while. I couldn't connect with her.

"Well, why did you do it?" I finally asked.

"I couldn't be on Earth anymore. I needed to leave. I didn't want to be there."

"You missed him a lot. I know," I said.

"I made a mistake though. You see, I have learned on the Other Side, that we all come to Earth to learn things. We have soul contracts that we form before we come to Earth that dictate what we are to learn and master on the Earth. When we take our own life, we are skipping out on that. We aren't showing up for what our soul expects of us. Even people that come to Earth and seem to struggle or fail, even people that suffer greatly on Earth—they are sent here with a purpose that is divinely granted. I didn't carry out my whole purpose on Earth. I didn't learn everything. But guess what? I'm learning a ton over here."

"You seem to be doing very well. How did you learn all of this?"

"You just know things—a lot of things—when you are over here. You just know them with absolute certainty. When you cross over, you become all knowing."

"I see."

"I'm going back now. Back over to the Other Side."

"Are we good? You and I?" I asked.

"We're perfect."

As I reflected on that day, I thought about how some-times "the gift" gets in the way and how, ultimately, a reading can do only so much. A powerful reading can educate and enlighten people about their destiny and life's hidden mean-ings. It can help people prepare for where they are going and what they will do. But sometimes in the midst of all the little messages, the biggest ones go unnoticed. I reminded myself: I heard Daisy out, and I helped her as best I could. I knew in my heart that no matter what came through in that read-ing—no matter what Spirit I channeled and what messages I delivered—Daisy would still have ended her life two days later. I could not change that, and I knew I should not enter-tain any guilt over what had happened.

A person's destiny is clearly his or her own and there is nothing that you—or I or anyone—can do to change it. May-be Daisy didn't know what she was doing. Yes, she had been planning her suicide *before* Justin's death. His death was just the icing on her irony cake. Perhaps she hadn't intended to trick me, and she definitely had *not* duped me. Maybe she really needed to be reassured that there was something more, such a place as Heaven. I finally understood the profundity of those words, now echoing in my mind, uttered by Daisy during that fateful reading: "We are here to learn what we had forgotten."

# CHAPTER 15

# WANTED: DEAD OR ALIVE

"Death is the veil which those who live call life; they sleep, and it is lifted."

—Percy Bysshe Shelley

"And who is Ron? I'm seeing the letters R–O–N." I said confidently, as I rolled up my shirtsleeves, my eyes closed. A male Spirit had just come forth—I could visualize him somewhat—a tall white-haired man; an angular face with big dimples. He seemed happy, but anxious, with a mysterious smile on his face. He was coming through strongly, giving me information so quickly that it was hard for me to keep up with him. I had a warm feeling around my neck like the gentle touch of a loving, but silent, grandfather's hand.

A medium is often mistaken as someone who sees ghosts and dead people. And while I do see dead people, I also see images, smell scents, and hear sounds that immediately relate to the person. And while that is certainly part of my work, being a medium is like playing a strange, dizzying, game of charades. I have visions of people, places, and things that are more akin to snapshots or a montage of scenes from a movie. Usually, the images, senses, and ideas that I receive relate to only one possible person in the Spirit World who has come forth to connect with the person being read. Sometimes, the information is clear and concise. At other times, it is nebulous and hazy. Being a medium, I sometimes feel like a detective. In this case, the Spirit showed me a chalkboard and rapidly wrote, in barely legible handwriting, his messages on it. After a few boards full of words, I finally was able to decipher the word "checkers." My job is not just sitting around chatting with dead folks.

Ronna Katzberg, the seventy-seven-year-old eccentric woman I was reading, was curled up across from me with her knees tucked up toward her stomach on a leather chaise with cherry legs, which she volunteered her great grandmother had passed down to her. She was thin with straight, reddish, closely cropped hair and was overly dressed for the occasion—jewelry on every finger; a thick black, cashmere sweater; tan pants that stopped at her ankles, with pink toenails that peeked out from three-inch black heels. An elaborate peacock broach was clasped above her breast. Long earrings, which sparkled in the light like icicles in the morning sun, dangled an inch above her shoulder, while her sweater hid her neck.

"Do checkers mean anything to you?" I asked her. I opened my eyes to see her response.

"That goes with my husband—he loves checkers! This is so cool. Do it again!" she screamed with enthusiasm. Her voice was high-pitched and child-like. "I just love him," she squealed while kicking her feet in the air a bit. She puckered her lips, smothered with pink gloss, and blew a kiss into the air. I watched her hands squeeze the arm of the leather chaise as her foot tapped anxiously against the arms of the chair.

That was a "hit," a term psychic mediums use to refer to a piece of information validated by the person being read. When I made this hit, her foot stopped tapping for a moment—as if she was caught off guard—and then the tapping began again. I then had several more hits come through, all of which she connected with her husband. I told her that I was hearing about Max, and she said that he was her husband's grandfather, whom he had loved dearly and to whom he was very close.

"I'm hearing that I am supposed to bring up something about Tootsie Rolls."

"Wow—where are you getting this from?" she asked. "Yes, on our wedding day, we ate a Tootsie Roll together in the morning for good luck; it was a strange superstitious ritual that he had done before all of his exams in dental school. I thought it was the weirdest thing, but looking back, it was so charming. Our whole marriage, Tootsie Rolls were always a sign of 'I love you.'" She stopped for a moment, and in a deeper, brooding voice, she boomed, "Are you reading my mind?" and then burst into a laughing fit that sounded like a hyena. "I bet you get that a lot T—Tommy Boy!" she stammered.

The room was filled with an odd collection of furniture—a cornucopia of modern pieces she told me that she had purchased in SoHo last summer when she decided to redecorate, as well as older pieces that were family heirlooms with which she could not part. "I just love stuff—old, new, and blue—like a wedding," she squealed when she gave me a small tour of her place upon my arrival. Everything was mismatched; the color combinations were completely out of sync. Dark blue drapes with red and pink fabrics, as well as heavy animal prints across the furniture pieces as blankets and throws. It reminded me of an installment by Yayoi Kusama. Several bookcases lined the wall, jam packed with books of all sizes, with no apparent organization. It seemed as though someone had started organizing some shelves but then stopped before finishing. The disarray made me feel uneasy and slightly claustrophobic.

This is one reason I don't like making house calls. I prefer to do readings in my own space. First, I don't like traveling. Even a trip on the subway makes me overwhelmed. I'm an anxious person by nature, and when I am traveling, I become even more so. Some would say I'm agoraphobic, I guess; but in my opinion, I'm just a creature of habit. Also, because I'm a psychic and a medium, I'm extra sensitive and pick up on the energy and emotions of everyone around me, so situations like elevators, escalators, or big crowds are fairly difficult. Similarly, I try to keep everything the same across readings—the same preparation, the same rituals. When the company that manufactured the perfect candles I used in my office went out of business two years ago, I was frantic for a month trying to find the proper replacement. The reason I do this is that I want to give the purest reading possible. Similar to a scientist who would want to test samples in his Petri dishes under equal conditions, I want to give my readings in similar environments. I want to know that what I perceive is actually connected with the Spirit and the person I am reading or their environment. However, I made an exception for Ronna. Not only had I known her mother, Pearl, but she was also a dear friend of a client of mine, whom I cared for deeply. Ronna asked for a reading but sometimes got confused traveling alone in the city. When she phoned for an appointment, coincidentally, I was already planning a trip to Scarsdale in two weeks to visit a close cousin of mine, whom I had not seen in several years. So I was able to accommodate her request for a house call.

"And why would your husband's Spirit be telling me about candy canes?" I continued. I had just been shown several candy canes and even had the fleeting, faint taste of plastic mixed with stale mint in my mouth.

"Oh, Ronnie loves candy canes. Even though we're Jews, we buy them every year at Christmas. He likes the mint ones and the cherry ones the best."

"Do you know who J is? A woman? Is it—Judy?"

"That's his mother! She's gone now. Let me tell you, that old bag never bought us a thing! But she was fat, and she loved to cook. The first time I met her, she wore all red, head to toe red. And trust me, we didn't get good seats at the symphony, even though she always made sure that *she* did. I hated her, but I loved her, but she didn't do a damned thing for me," Ronna said, her sentences running together. It was sometimes tough to follow her train of thought or even understand her words.

It is common for Spirits that are a bit surprising to come through. Your nasty ex-mother-in-law, your dead boyfriend from high school, or your friend's dog—all can be possible suspects for the Spirit that comes through in a reading. When I open myself up to the Spirit World, I'm merely the messenger. Sometimes people get selected to be a messenger in their own readings. You might get a message for someone else with whom you aren't that close; nonetheless, Spirit has chosen you to relay a message to them. Beloved, or even bemoaned, Spirits want us to know as much as they do, and be a part of our lives.

"Your husband is telling me he is sorry for passing so suddenly. He said it was quick, and he was not in pain," I reassured her. It is common for Spirits to bring up their deaths in reading.

*"Passing?"* she shouted. She had just thrown a handful of almonds into her mouth as I said this, and sat frozen, mid-chew. A very puzzled look came over her face.

"Yes, passing. His death," I said quietly.

"Oh, I'm sorry. You must be confused. Ronnie isn't dead. We're meeting at Pepinos after we're done. It's martini n . . . ," she started choking on an almond. "It's martini night."

I felt a pain in my heart and then rapid beating. I began to sweat. "But he's sitting right here talking to me."

"Ronnie is?"

"Yes, I am speaking with him." I tuned back immediately and I heard, "It's me. I'm Ronnie." It was, indeed, Ronnie. I was puzzled.

"Well, you can't be! He's alive. Maybe it's his dad. His father was Robert. I never knew him, but I think they were a lot alike," she said laughing it off, trying to be nice. Sometimes people try to make what comes through in their reading fit their purposes. "An R for an R!" she screamed.

Now, if there is one thing I know, it's dead people. I've been around as many as a coroner. I've spoken to thousands of Spirits. Young ones, old ones, new ones, and fifty-years-dead ones. I've spoken to the Spirits of dogs, cats, birds, and once, the Spirit of a goat (that was a little weird). The messages they bring through are all unique. Sometimes they speak words of comfort in order to help loved ones struggling on this side. Sometimes they are at unrest and need closure before they can make a full transition. Other times, it's a drive-by reading: hello and good-bye. But I know what I am getting. This is real to me and to the people I am sitting with. There's no way I could mistake someone's husband for dead if they were still living. I do not get significant things, such as this, wrong.

But doubt is a tricky, nasty beast. And to be fair, I think Ronna would know if her husband of fifty-seven years were dead. Denial may be blind, but it's not deaf. Sometimes my clients deny the messages that come through: for example, a mother's Spirit apologizes for being an alcoholic, but her adult child never admits that the mother was an alcoholic, so she can't wrap her mind around it.

Perhaps my wires were crossed. I picked up on the energy of a living person and brought him through as a dead person? Waiter! Check, please. I tried to stay positive. Fact started blurring with fiction as my imagination went wild. Was Ronna fantasizing that her husband was alive? Had he actually died years ago, and she refused to accept it? I suddenly wanted to excuse myself to sneak a peek in the master bedroom. Was

Ronnie propped up in the bed, his corpse rotting, the smell masked by cleaning chemicals? I had to retune my senses; I could feel the reading slipping away. I felt sick to my stomach; a pain radiated down my spine. I was embarrassed, stressed, and extremely confused. My ears were ringing. I thought to myself, *If I'm wrong, how many other times has this happened? How many other times had I perfectly described someone's late mother who was alive and well in Florida? Or someone's dead son who worked two jobs to support his wife and three kids? Or someone's late grandfather who was slowing down at ninety-four, but not dead? Were some people just scared to tell me?*

I had to separate from my ego, the part of me that needed to be right. I took a deep breath. I excused myself to go to the bathroom. I needed some space to quiet my mind. I washed my hands. The sink, like most of the furnishings in Ronna's home, was mismatched and out of place. The basin was shiny metal, held up by a black vanity post, with no counter space. It appeared it was placed haphazardly with no regard to functionality. I stared blankly into the mirror in front of me. It was housed in a golden brass frame that featured a dragon relief with red stones in the eyes. They stared at me as if to say, "Phony! You're nothing but a sham. Loser! You're a freak show." I moved my eyes away and stared at my own reflection. My face was flushed, and I was nauseous. I started coughing; dry heaves filled my chest, and I thought I would vomit.

I looked up in the mirror. "Is he dead?" I asked, desperate for an answer. I got the feeling I had to return and face my client.

When I returned, Ronna was sitting where I had left her, her glass of water was refilled and she held a sketchpad in her lap. Ironically, I sensed that my blunder somehow got her more interested in the reading than she was at the beginning.

"I'm sorry about—" I started to apologize but was interrupted. "Are you kidding? I'm having a great time," she said. She begged me to continue, clapping her hands together as if to cheer me on.

I watched her doodle in the pad while maintaining eye contact with me. "I never mess up like that. I don't want to scare you." My head pulsated and my eyes throbbed.

"Let's get on with it. Who else can you bring into the reading? I'm ready; let's go!"

I did as she requested. A dizzying number of Spirits came through, including her late mother who had many tidbits to share with her only child. The two of them caught up like old friends at a high school reunion. Then her grandmother materialized, and I was shown a car accident involving two people. Ronna was excited, and validated that her grandmother and her best friend, Eliza, had passed together in a car accident when her mother was only nineteen.

She furiously wrote notes, hanging onto every word, immediately jotting down any name, place, or date I mentioned on her legal pad like a court reporter. When she filled one page, she tore if off and threw it into the air, albeit dramatically, to scurry onto the next page. I wasn't talking very fast, but she wrote quickly, as if someone had made a bet with her that she couldn't transcribe all my words before I spoke them.

At one point, she ran out of ink, squiggling neurotically on the pad to make the pen work.

I channeled for another thirty minutes and then began to lose my ability to connect with the other side. When I looked up at Ronna, she winked.

"Well, that was really something!" she said, rising from the chaise lounge. When she bent over, her pants clenched so tightly around her hips, it looked as if they might split in two. She thanked me for making the trip to Scarsdale as we walked toward the front door. I felt numb and empty inside. Depleted.

As if reading my mind, Ronna said, "And don't worry about your thinking Ronnie was dead—how funny though! I wonder what I would do if he croaked!" She laughed as a snort escaped from her nose. "I know how it is. You people aren't God!" She slapped me on the back, like a coach would his star quarterback who just fumbled the ball. I kept my composure, but deep down inside, I was angry. She was laughing at me, and it made me feel small and insignificant.

I made my way down the winding staircase that led to the driveway where I'd parked my car. I was afraid to look back toward the house, and worried that if I did, I'd be met with Ronna's deep-set eyes staring, maybe even smirking, at me.

On the way home, I cried. I felt so defeated. Thoughts raced through my head. Should I leave the psychic world altogether? How long would it take me to pack up my office? Could I enroll at NYU? What would I study? Would Ronna tell her friends about the funny quack psychic who couldn't tell who was dead and who was alive? Would people laugh at me? A horn beeped in the lane next to me. In my daze, I was shifting lanes without realizing it. I was driving back to Chelsea, on the west side, but somehow in my confusion I took a wrong turn and ended up on the east side. I continued driving and exited FDR Drive. Going across town, I almost hit a woman and her shopping cart. I pulled over on 2nd Avenue at 19th Street to calm myself down, and just sat for a moment with my hazards blinking. After I was a bit more relaxed, I gathered my thoughts and drove my car extra slow to the garage and went for a long run.

The next week, I received a voicemail from Ronna. She said she wanted to schedule a follow-up reading, and it was important that I phone her back as soon as possible. I wasn't surprised; it's common for people to enjoy their session and want a second one immediately as more and more questions seem to pop up. My assistant returned her call but got her answering machine. She thanked Ronna for reaching out but explained that I usually read people only once every six months. Frequent readings can make a person too dependent on them and the Spirits' information. That evening, as I was packing my briefcase to leave the office, I saw Ronna's number on the caller ID for the office landline. I knew we had already called her back, but I answered, which was unlike me at that late hour of the evening.

"It's Ronna. I have to speak with you immediately. Something's changed. It's very important."

"Something changed?"

"Yes. You see, when you read for me, you told me about Ronnie. Do you remember?"

"Of course," I said, as my embarrassment resurfaced. I felt my cheeks get thick and hot.

"Well, it turns out, Ronnie never showed up for dinner that night. I was scared, so I went to his office and found him dead on the floor. He was catching up on paperwork, alone. The coroner said he probably died that morning, a heart attack, and had been sitting there for some time. The office was closed, so nobody was there."

My head was spinning; my arms started to tremble. All of the hairs on my arms and neck stood up.

"So, I think when you were giving me my reading, it was him coming through trying to reach me. You see, he *was* dead. You were right." She began sobbing. Deep and guttural sobs. "I need to talk to him and see if he has any messages for me. I'm very worried about him, and I feel terrible that I ignored him during our reading."

It's hard to describe my feelings at that exact moment. Part of me felt vindicated. I felt relieved. I hadn't lost my mind. I wasn't wrong about something so important. But at the same time, I also felt sadness that we mistakenly ignored someone's Spirit eagerly trying to communicate his first message from the Spirit World. As Ronna cried, I glanced out at the street below. The Park Avenue traffic at 5 p.m., the sound of honking horns, and the sight of commuters rushing in the street. The street was alive as ever.

The weather was cold and brisk on the day of Ronna's second reading, exactly eleven days after her first reading. In my briefcase, I felt the heavy weight of the lilac candles from the

Namaste Bookshop and their smell wafted out of the bag to my nose. I had intended to take the day off, but made a special accommodation to meet Ronna at 9:00 a.m. I was running late, and when I arrived at my office, she was already there, pacing anxiously in the waiting room.

"Are you ready for me?" she asked, as I put the key into the doorknob.

"I'm almost ready. Just relax." As I said it, I caught myself. I sounded mean and rude, almost arrogant. My nerves were getting the better of me.

My lips were dry, my palms sweaty and clammy. I had goose bumps on my arms. Normally, I don't connect with newer Spirits because I find that the connection is better if I wait until at least two to three months after they have crossed over. But since Ron's Spirit had come forward in Ronna's first reading, I figured he was likely to make a second appearance. Plus, this reading would take place on my turf. Gone were the excessive decorations and loud colors. This time, my environment was calm and much more conducive to a successful reading. I should have been confident at least we knew who was dead and who wasn't.

When Ronna entered my office, she seemed different. Her demeanor was much more quiet and reserved. She was dressed simply. Instead of loud colors and excessive jewelry, she wore white pearls, a simple pair of earrings, and a black suit. She looked elegant and modest. At the first reading, she stared me down and gawked at everything I did. This time she couldn't even make eye contact. As she slowly walked toward the couch, it seemed as though her legs and body were aching; it reminded me of the way a sore runner walks after a grueling marathon. I lit a candle in front of me, my usual ritual, as I waited for her to finish her nervous fidgeting. She took out a pack of tissues and then placed them back in her purse. Then she removed them again and put them on the table between us. "Can I put these there?" she asked. I nodded, and for the first time, we made eye contact.

"You were right," she said. I cringed a bit at the words. They felt silly to me now. I wasn't trying to prove a point. I didn't want it to be that way. But somehow, I still felt relieved. I wondered if I was the first person in the history of the world who perhaps felt *less* crazy after being told that he was seeing invisible people.

A police siren trailing off in the distance added to my anxiety. Even though this time I knew the key players with whom Ronna wanted to connect, I was uneasy nonetheless.

Ronnie came through with ease. I could sense his excitement. He jumped from one topic to the next; he spoke about his death, then about his childhood. One moment he reminisced about their wedding day; the next he babbled about their daughter.

When I glanced at Ronna, her face was open. Her body was relaxed and her aura seemed quiet. There were no almonds being tossed in the air, no notes being taken, no jewelry-covered hands flailing about wildly. The connection with Ronnie was strong and emotional; he was even pushy, correcting me about what I communicated to Ronna. This time his presence was validated, and he was going to get his point across. In my head, I heard the words, "I want to be heard," like one of the speechless voices we sometimes hear echoing in our heads.

Ronnie talked about what he had done in the minutes and seconds before his death. He wanted the death part to be clear; I could tell by the way he was methodically going through each and every detail about his passing.

"He's telling me there wasn't any pain," I told her, as I put my hand on my chest. "He said he just felt weak and dropped." I felt light-headed.

"That's what I hoped for," she said.

"He didn't take care of himself always, even though he was a doctor," I blurted out. I had just had an instance of claircognizance, when I am not hearing anything or feeling anything specific, but suddenly just knew something, like an idea that pops into my head out of nowhere. I opened my eyes to see her reaction. I wanted to know if I was going too deep or if this was too emotional.

"He always put others first; he always neglected his own health," she said. She let out a sigh, as a tear rolled down her face.

"It's a common thing with men," I offered. I didn't like to coach or advise someone in this way, but I could sense her pain was fresh and new, and I wanted to console her.

"He's talking about the house; the back of the house, or the backyard?"

"What about it?" she looked out the window, trying to reflect and think about what her husband's Spirit was referencing.

"He's talking about something he buried out there; you two buried something?" He was now showing me a hole and some dirt around it. I saw a shovel digging into the ground.

"Oh, I forgot about that. Yes. We made a time capsule. Does he want me to open it up?"

A light flickered on the table.

"I heard something about a Susan, too?"

"There's no Susan that I know of," Ronna said. "But I will try to remember her." She wouldn't dare say no to a message now.

"He also said Jerome or Jerry?" I added.

"These names aren't making sense," Ronna said. "But I will make a note of them for sure."

We continued the reading well past 10 a.m., when the reading was scheduled to end. But Ronnie kept talking, so I kept channeling. I wasn't sure why exactly he was so loquacious, but it was obvious that he wanted to communicate with his wife.

By 10:30 a.m. I knew I had done enough. We had spent almost ninety minutes conversing with Ronnie; almost double one of my usual readings, which were scheduled in thirty- to sixty-minute slots. Strangely enough, I wasn't at all fatigued. Letting go of the energy surrounding Ronnie—the confusion, the questions, the back and forth—was both cleansing and relieving and even uplifting. But ninety minutes was enough. I wanted to let him go back to the Spirit World where he belonged. It is not healthy for either the departed or their survivors to connect too often. The dead need to acclimate to their new state of being, something that constant communication with the people left behind does not facilitate. But I brought through one last message about Ronnie's transition before we ended. He wanted to let Ronna know that he had encountered some of her family members on the other side, even distant relatives that had passed away long before Ronnie and Ronna exchanged their first Tootsie Roll.

"No, keep going," Ronna said, wiping her eyes with a tissue. "I need to hear more. I don't care what it takes—I want more." Her voice was gentle and soft and didn't match her strong demands.

"I think it's really a good idea to stop here. We're way over on time, and it's hard for me to stay connected too long," I said. "When I do, the information can become inaccurate."

She let out a sigh. "Okay, I trust you. I can always come back, right?"

"Yes, of course," I confirmed.

"I can't thank you enough; somehow it's helpful to know that they are around us. It makes you think, really," she said. "I feel like we've been through the war together, you and I."

"It sure has been an experience." I forced a smile.

We both sat there. Silently. The clock on my wall ticked loudly.

"Ronnie, I'm sorry," she blurted out to no one in particular. Then she turned to me and asked, "Can they hear us when we talk to them?"

I nodded. "They're just a thought away."

"I'm sorry, Ronnie. I'm sorry I didn't listen to you when you tried to talk to me. But I know you're okay now. I love you bubalah." She smiled a bit. "You know, I thought it would be fun to connect like this—and it was—but it's a really emotional experience, isn't it?"

"Yes," I said simply. I put my hand over my chin.

She hoisted herself out of her seat, grabbing the sides of the chair for assistance. She did the same with the walls as she walked toward the exit, as if she were drunk or exhausted and unable to maintain her balance. She seemed less of a person since Ronnie's death, as if only a part of her still remained. She also looked physically diminutive now, whereas before her presence was larger than life. As she made her way to the elevator, she seemed weak and broken. Darkness surrounded her eyes, a grayish color, as if she had painted a cloudy, rainy sky above her cheekbones.

As I closed the door behind her, a sense of calm swept over me. I let out a deep breath and rested my body against the back of the door. My head was pounding. My heart started beating more slowly. I breathed in a deep breath and exhaled. For the past week, I had felt tired and irritable—I had snapped so many times, so frequently. I was on edge even before Ronna had informed me that Ronnie was dead, and I still was after I found out.

I looked outside. Heavy rain began to pour on the city. It was refreshing in a way, as if it were disinfecting my space from the awkward situation that Ronna and I had experienced over the past two weeks. We had a fresh start now. I realized now that my depression, the darkness and the heaviness, was most likely due to Ronnie's lingering presence and his confusion about how his widow had ignored his message. Now, he had fully transitioned to the other side and was ready to embark on a new path and learn new lessons. He was at peace. We all were.

# ABOUT THE AUTHOR

Thomas John is an up-and-coming psychic medium and clairvoyant who has conducted thousands of readings around the world. He has been referred to as "the must-see celebrity psychic of NYC" by *Hollywoodlife.com*. He has made numerous appearances in the media, including *Dr. Phil*, and has had dozens of features in the *Wall Street Journal*, *New York* magazine, *OK!* magazine, the *New York Post*, and the *Hollywood Reporter*. He is active on the lecture circuit, and his client list includes Courtney Cox, Julianne Moore, Stevie Nicks, and Goldie Hawn. Website: *www.mediumthomas.com*

# HAMPTON ROADS PUBLISHING COMPANY

*. . . for the evolving human spirit*

Hampton Roads Publishing Company publishes books on a variety of subjects, including spirituality, health, and other related topics.

For a copy of our latest trade catalog, call (978) 465-0504 or visit our distributor's website at *www.redwheelweiser.com.* You can also sign up for our newsletter and special offers by going to *www.redwheelweiser.com/newsletter/.*